THE ARCHAEOLOGY OF THE
NORTHEAST MOJAVE DESERT

Gary B. Coombs

with contributions by

Robert H. Crabtree and Elizabeth Warren

Prepared by Archaeological Research, Inc. for the
United States Department of the Interior, Bureau of
Land Management under contract YA-512-CT7-236: A
Class II Cultural Resources Inventory of the
Bitterwater, Kingston and northern half of the
Owlshead/Amargosa Planning Units, California
Desert.

Eric W. Ritter
General Editor

1979

Kingston Range, Inyo County, California. View north toward
California and Pahrump valleys.

FORWARD

By publishing this report the Bureau of Land Management in California has taken a positive step in the dissemination of important archaeological data to both the public and the profession. This is a study which combines management and research objectives into an informative package concerning a relatively unknown region of the United States.

For over a decade now the Bureau of Land Management has been involved in the California Desert Study Program. This program developed as a response to the many demands increasingly being placed on the California Desert by various user groups. Cultural resources are an important and integral part of this study. A major goal of the program is the completion of an implementable multiple use plan for the California Desert, and a principal objective is the preservation and protection of cultural resources. Toward this end numerous archaeological and historical studies have been undertaken, both by Bureau personnel and outside contractors. Detailed cultural resource overviews have been completed as the first step. Such overviews synthesize regional archaeological, ethnological, ethnohistorical and historical data, discuss past and projected research, highlight significant cultural/environmental interrelationships, and identify management and research questions and needs. Subsequent field inventories, such as detailed here, provide the next step in the process. When all the data is eventually pulled together there will be a package available to assist land managers in their role as caretakers of the desert and to aid cultural resources specialists in future work.

This report goes beyond the usual site survey presentation to offer important insights into questions regarding site survey validity and reliability. The actual survey strategy is innovative considering the various constraints imposed on the contractor. The results of the work exceed what was expected and have significant implications to other workers in arid environments, to land managers, and to the public who enjoy learning of the past activities of the various peoples who utilized this land. Nevertheless, this study can be considered no more than setting the stage for further and perhaps even more exciting and informative work.

Eric W. Ritter
General Editor

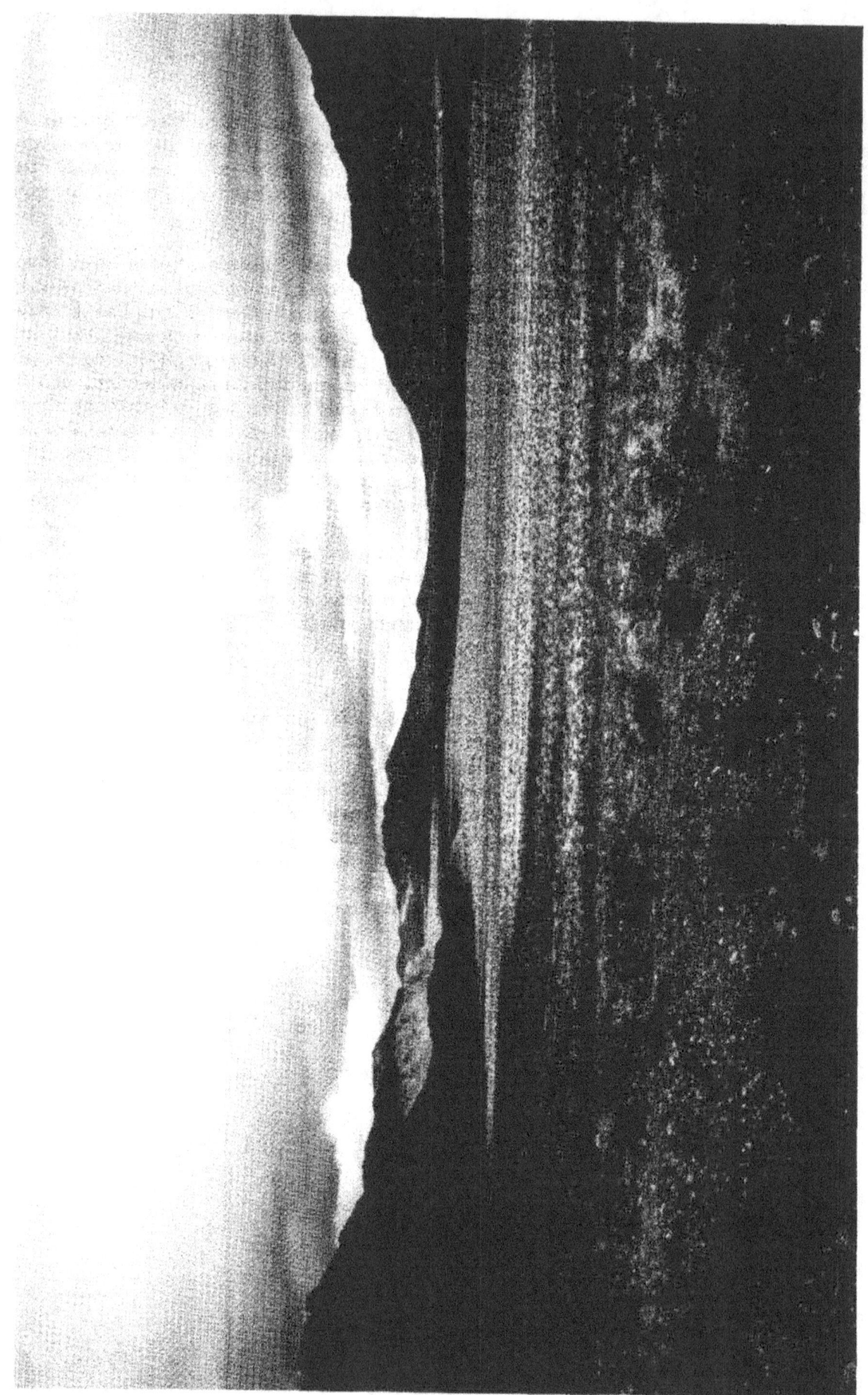

Chicago Valley, Inyo County, California. View north toward
Resting Spring and Nopah ranges.

CONTENTS

Page

Preface   ii

1. General Information   1

2. The Natural Environment   6
        Robert H. Crabtree

3. Cultural Historical Review   18
        Robert H. Crabtree and Elizabeth Warren,
        assisted by Tara Shepperson

4. Sampling Design   29

5. Field Implementation   46

6. Validity and Reliability   58

7. Results   76

8. Site Evaluation and Recommendations   119
        Gary Coombs and Robert H. Crabtree

References   132

Appendix I: BLM Site Classification System   141

PREFACE

This report is concerned with the results of an archaeological survey of approximately 17,000 acres in the northeastern portion of the Mojave Desert. For readers unfamiliar with the term, an archaeological survey (or inventory) generally consists of an on-foot reconnaissance of a given area, in search of archaeological sites located on the surface of the ground. The survey includes the reconnaissance itself, together with the recording of site and other information. The Northeast Mojave survey covered 1% of the total surface area within that region.

The research was conducted by Archaeological Research, Inc. under contract YA-512-CT7-236 with the U.S. Department of the Interior, Bureau of Land Management, as part of the Bureau's California Desert Planning Program.

This report is intended primarily as a management and research tool. It was originally written specifically for the BLM Desert Planning Staff, to aid them in the preparation of a plan, required by law, for the protection and use of the California Desert. Since the research led to a number of important findings concerning the prehistory and history of the Northeast Mojave, the report is addressed, secondarily, to professional anthropologists and historians interested in this particular area, or similar areas or peoples in other parts of the world.

Other readers, those less-versed in the jargon of management and anthropology, will therefore find many portions of this report to be highly technical, uninformative, or simply boring. Hopefully, this type of reader can overcome these obstacles and benefit from the remainder of the report.

I am personally pleased that members of the general public will have access to this report, not only because the research was funded with tax-payer dollars but also because the report documents an aspect of the heritage of all of us. It should thus be of at least some interest and significance to almost everyone.

Unfortunately, open access has its liabilities and dangers as well. Our research led to a number of highly sensitive findings, particularly with regard to the specific locations of a large number of archaeological sites. Unscrupulous individuals have been known to use the published accounts of such information to locate and loot sites, despite the federal, state and local laws which prohibit such activities. To hinder this misuse, I have made every effort to avoid identifying site locations in the published version of this report.

The report contains eight chapters and several appendices. Chapter 1 is a general introduction and includes preliminary information concerning the project area, the motivating forces behind the research and its objectives and conduct. Chapters 2 and 3 contain more specific data concerning the environment and cultural history, respectively, of the Northeast Mojave. Chapter 4 discusses the procedures used in selecting the areal sample used in the inventory, and outlines the rationale behind this selection. Chapter 5 describes the methods used in conducting the inventory itself, including logistical procedures and problems, recording techniques, and so on. Chapter 6 examines, in detail, potential problems which may arise in efforts to interpret the results of the research, including questions of validity and reliability in sampling, measurement, and analysis.

The results of the analysis portion of the research are outlined in Chapter 7, which deals principally with site density estimates and observed spatial relationships between arhcaeological site types and select environmental variables such as vegetation and water resources. Chapter 8 contains a series of recommendations, based upon the research, for the protection of archaeological resources in the Northeast Mojave and for their use in future research and education.

The published appendix consists of the BLM Site Classification System utilized in the recording and typing of sites. All subsequent appendices contain site-location and other particularly sensitive data which could lead to the vandalism of sites, and do not appear in the published version of this report.

This report would not have been possible without the invaluable efforts of a number of people. Through rain, wind, cold and loose sand, Bob Crabtree somehow supervised the fieldwork through to its completion, and still had enough time and energy to make several written contributions to this volume. Consultants to the research, paid and otherwise, included Claude Warren, Sr. (prehistory), Richard Arnold (Native American culture), Margaret Lyneis (sampling), Liz Warren (history), Dave Weide (geology), and Joe King (botany). Fieldworkers were Richard McCarty, Tara Shepperson, Scott Crownover, Claude Warren, Jr., Evan Crabtree, Mike Plyler, Dan Tublitz, Kevin August, Kelli Greene, Linda Abernathy, Pat Baratti and Lou Hensen. The office staff consisted of Kelli Greene, who typed, edited, reviewed, coded and plotted, and finished what fieldwork the rest of us left undone.

Contracting Officer for the BLM, Darrell Mahlik, gave invaluable advice on how to run a business to someone who wasn't quite sure and, in making certain that the checks arrived on time, kept all of us going. The Contracting Officer's Authorized Representative, Eric Ritter, of the BLM Desert Planning Staff, provided technical direction essential to the research, and has been patient and tolerant above and beyond the call of duty.

This list would not be complete without mentioning the most crucial contributors to the research: the past peoples of the Northeast Mojave. To those who fought an unforgiving environment, this report is dedicated.

G.C.
Santa Barbara, California
September, 1978

CHAPTER 1. GENERAL INTRODUCTION

A. Background

Under the Federal Land Policy and Management Act of 1976
(Public Law 94-579), the United States Department of the Interior,
Bureau of Land Management was mandated to prepare, by October 1,
1980, a land use allocation plan for the California Desert Conservation Area. The California Desert was specifically identified in
the Act because of its delicate nature from an environmental standpoint and because it is an area which is "seriously threatened by
air pollution, inadequate Federal management authority, and pressures
of increased use, particularly recreational use, which are certain
to intensify because of the rapidly growing population of Southern
California."

Among other considerations, the Act points out the need to
identify, evaluate and protect the archaeological, historic and
cultural resources lying within the California Desert Conservation
Area. More generally, these same requirements are mandated under
the Antiquities Act of 1906, the Reservoir Salvage Act of 1960, as
amended, the National Environmental Policy Act of 1969 and Executive
Order 11593.

In order to meet the October 1980 deadline, the Bureau of Land
Management (BLM) elected to address cultural resource concerns on a
regional basis and to secure independent contractors to aid in the
completion of a portion of the cultural resource investigation.

The study of each Desert region would be divided further, into
two parts: 1) a "Class I" Inventory, consisting of a review of
existing written and other data sources, and; 2) a "Class II" Inventory, consisting of an original field inventory (sample) and resulting
report.

The basic objectives of the Class II Inventories are:

1) to identify and evaluate, from surface and exposed profile indications, all cultural resource sites within a (sampled) portion
   of the defined region;

2) to estimate, by means of statistical analysis and other methods,
   the nature and distribution of all cultural resources within
   the total region;

3) to identify the environmental and/or cultural/historical variables, or combination of variable, that may be used to predict
   the dispersion and diversity of cultural resources in the defined
   region; and

4) to provide, through field work, analysis and report preparation,
   a sound basis for making planning decisions concerning cultural
   resources in said region.

B. Project Area

On September 30, 1977, the BLM awarded Archaeological Research, Inc. a contract to conduct a Class II Inventory of the Kingston, Bitterwater, and northern half of the Owlshead/Amargosa Planning Units, California Desert. This area is most easily and aptly labelled the Northeast Mojave Desert region (see Figure 1-1).

The Bitterwater Planning Unit is bounded on the west by Death Valley National Monument, on the north and east by the California-Nevada border, and on the south by the Inyo-San Bernardino County Line. The northern half of the Owlshead/Amargosa Planning Unit is bounded on the north by Death Valley National Monument and the Inyo-San Bernardino County line, on the west by the U.S. Ordnance Test Station and Camp Irwin Military Reservation, and includes the upper 1/3 of township 17 North in the south. The Kingston Planning Unit is bounded on the east by the California-Nevada border, on the north by the Inyo-San Bernardino County Line, and on the south by Interstate Highway 15.

Approximately 1.7 million acres (over 1.6% of the state) lie within the project domain and, among other requirements, the contract called for an intensive survey of 1% of this total area. Thus, in terms of both overall area and survey area, the project represents one of the largest cultural resource inventories ever to be undertaken in the State of California.

C. Archaeological Research, Inc. (ARI)

Archaeological Research, Inc. is an independent, non-profit organization dedicated to the further understanding and preservation of American cultures, both past and present, through anthropological research, publication, and education. Founded in 1968, ARI is the oldest anthropological corporation on the West Coast, deriving its funding from contracts, grants and private contributions.

During its history, ARI has completed research projects for the Bureau of Land Management, Bureau of Reclamation, National Park Service, Atomic Energy Commission, Department of Health, Education and Welfare, U.S. Geological Survey, California Department of Transportation, a number of California cities and counties, and a variety of other public and private agencies.

As a non-profit organization, Archaeological Research, Inc. maintains contractual and other relationships with the University of California and the University of Nevada for the use of library and laboratory facilities, and other services. ARI is an Associate member of the Santa Barbara Museum of Natural History and is affiliated, through its Directors, with the American Association for the Advancement of Science, American Anthropological Association, Society for American Archaeology and a number of other scientific organizations.

D. ARID-I

    For simplicity, the project with which this report is concerned
was designated "ARID-I." The name accurately reflects the climate
of the area in question, but also stands for Archaeological Research,
Inc. Desert Inventory. The name also fortuitously anticipated the
subsequent award of two additional desert inventory contracts from
the BLM. The first of these, a Class I Overview, thus received the
label "ARID-O" (for ARI Desert Overview), while the second, another
Class II Inventory, logically became "ARID-II."

E. Contract Requirements

    A number of specific project features were required under the
ARID-I contract. In large part, these basic requirements and other
guidelines were designed to help insure that the methods employed
and the data generated by the BLM and its contractors in different
desert areas would be comparable; this comparability of methods
and data was considered essential to the development of an overall
Desert Plan. Since the sampling design and many other aspects of
this research are understandable only in terms of these requirements and guidelines, it is useful to devote some space to a brief
review.

    The following includes those contract specifications most
directly affecting the nature of ARID-I and thus those most critical
to the interpretation of the balance of this report.

1) The inventory was to consist of an intensive survey of 1% (16,640
    acres) of the project area.

2) The survey was to be implemented in a minimum of two chronologi-
    cal stages, with later stages designed to amplify and test pre-
    dictions and projections derived from the first stage. Approxi-
    mately 2/3 of the survey was to be included in Stage I, the
    remaining 1/3 in subsequent stages.

3) The survey was to involve a stratified random sample, utilizing
    select environmental variables (e.g. vegetation, geomorphology,
    water resources) considered to be meaningful in relation to
    prehistoric and historic activities, as sampling strata.

4) The 1% sample was to be divided into a minimum of 208 "sample
    units" or "transects."

5) Each sample unit would be 1/8 mile wide and 1 mile long, and
    oriented either north-south or east-west so as to conform to
    the existing cadastral (i.e. land ownership, or township-section)
    grid.

6) Sample units were to be covered on foot, utilizing 4 evenly-
    spaced sweeps (see Figure 5-1) whenever possible.

7) The classification of all archaeological sites was to be based
    upon the BLM Site Classification System (Appendix I).

8) Site recordation and the recording of environmental and other sample unit data were to utilize existing BLM Site and Sample Unit Record Forms (Figures 5-3 through 5-5).

9) Site recordation was to be based on surface and exposed profile indications exclusively: sub-surface probing was not permitted.

10) In general, all aspects of the research, including sample design development, fieldwork, analysis and reporting, were to be geared to the further elucidation of archaeological potential, significance and sensitivity within the project area.

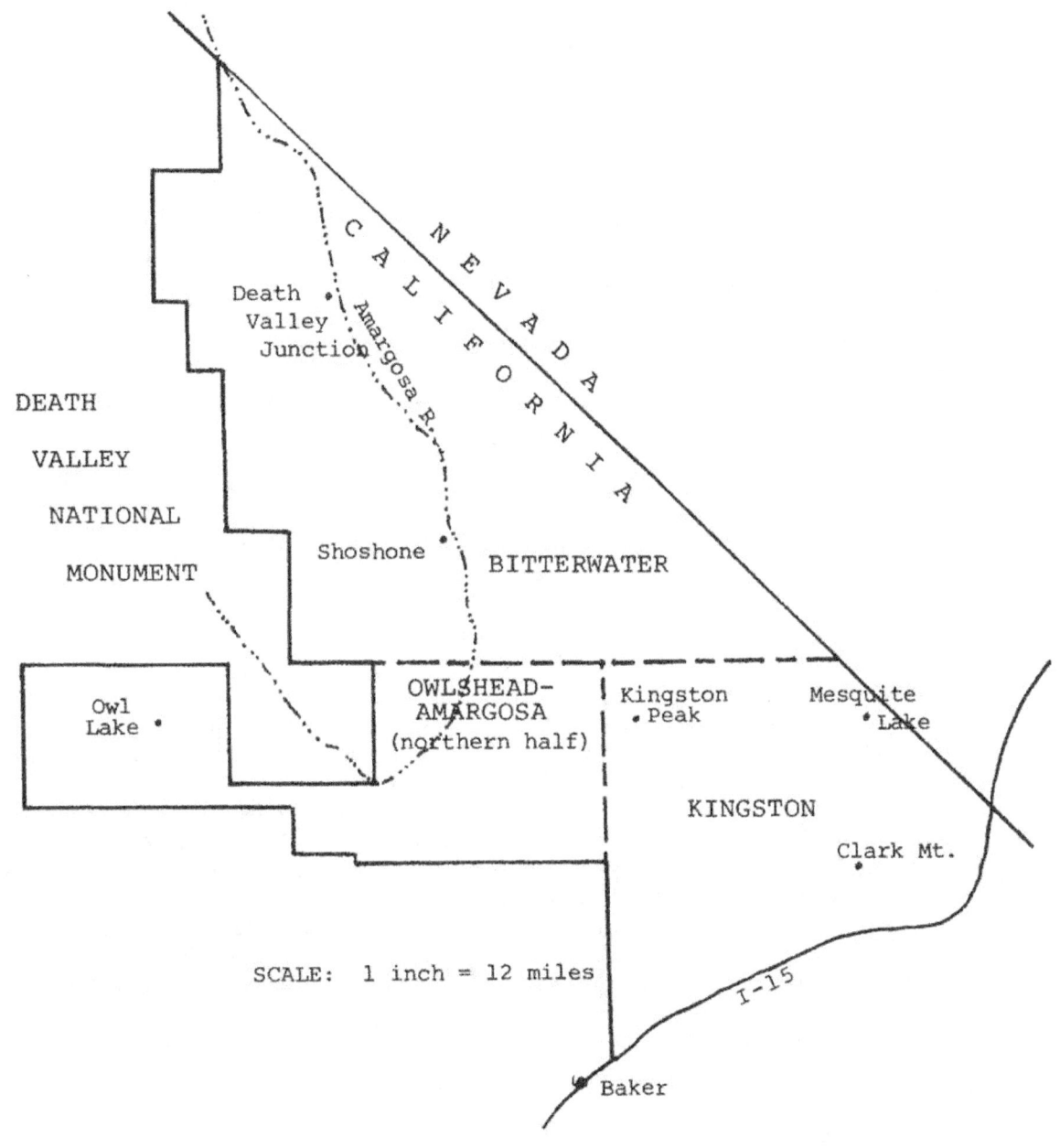

FIGURE 1-1.

THE NORTHEAST MOJAVE REGION

CHAPTER 2. THE NATURAL ENVIRONMENT

Robert H. Crabtree

The Mojave Desert, which constitutes a large section of the basin-and-range physiographic province defined by Fenneman (1931), is an arid region of internal drainage lying in the southeastern portion of the State of California. The ARID-I project area, which covers approximately 2650 square miles, lies in the northeastern quarter of the Mojave, coinciding in large part (but not exclusively) with the drainage system of the Amargosa River.

Among the environmental factors important to an understanding of past human activity in the project area, and thus to the evaluation of existing cultural resources, the following are perhaps particularly crucial: topography, climate, water resources, flora and fauna. In treating physiography and water resources, I find it convenient to divide the Northeast Mojave into five discrete sub-areas. Following this, I will discuss climatic and biotic characteristics on a more general, area-wide level.

A. Owlshead Mountains Sub-Area

The Owlshead Mountains sub-area lies directly west of the southern end of Death Valley and is the westernmost segment of the study area. It is dominated by the Owlshead Mountains, a series of ridges oriented in a roughly circular pattern around two playa basins, Owl Lake (517 m. above sea level) and Lost Lake (712 m. above sea level). Peaks in the Owlshead Range extend from about 1000 to over 1500 meters above sea level. The southwestern corner of this sub-area contains a portion of the Quail Mountains which also rise to over 1500 meters above sea level. The eastern portion of this sub-area drains directly into the Amargosa River in the southern part of Death Valley. The remainder of the sub-area also drains into the Amargosa River and Death Valley, but by a more circuitous route south and west of the Quail Mountains into Panamint Valley, and eventually into Death Valley by way of Wingate Wash.

B. The Amargosa Desert Sub-Area

The northern half (approximately) of the project area consists of the southern end of the Amargosa Desert, a basin flanked by several northwest-southeast trending mountain ranges. This portion of the Amargosa Desert contains the Amargosa River, a series of washes which in pluvial times served as overflow channels for Pahrump Valley to the east. North of Eagle Mountain and east of Death Valley Junction, the Amargosa River has as many as eight parallel channels (all of which may carry runoff water during periods of heavy rainfall), which empty into an extensive alkalai flat immediately north of Eagle Mountain. The Amargosa is flanked by the Black Mountains and the Greenwater Range, both composed of intrusive and extrusive rocks, primarily Cenozoic in origin.

Crestlines in the Greenwater Range vary from 1200 to over 1500 meters above sea level. Direct access routes into Greenwater Valley, to the west, from the Amargosa Desert, which lies between 600 and 700 meters above sea level, were available at Greenwater Canyon and Deadman Pass, both below 1200 meters elevation. The Black Mountains, at the western edge of this sub-area, are slightly more rugged and steeper than the Greenwater Range, and somewhat higher. The Funeral Mountains, north and west of the Amargosa Desert, and the Resting Springs and Nopah ranges of the eastern edge of the study area, are fault-block systems composed of sedimentary rocks of Late pre-Cambrian and Paleozoic times (Wright 1974). A noteworthy feature at the southern end of the Amargosa Desert sub-area is Eagle Mountain, an isolated fault-block mountain, similar in formation to the Resting Springs Range directly east, and rising abruptly nearly 600 meters from the valley floor to an elevation approximately 1200 meters above sea level. Lying between the Resting Springs and Nopah ranges is Chicago Valley, and just south of the Nopah Range is California Valley, both with elevations between 600 and 900 meters above sea level. The two ranges have crestlines varying from 1200 to 1500 meters above sea level in the Resting Springs Range and from 1200 to nearly 2000 meters above sea level in the Nopah Range. To the east of the Nopah Range is Pahrump Valley, which straddles the State boundary. In this same area are Mesquite Valley (called Sandy Valley in Nevada) and Stewart Valley, located at the southern and northern ends of Pahrump Valley, respectively. Elevations of the valley floors in this chain average slightly below 750 meters above sea level. These valleys each contain extensive playa or wash areas, relics of pluvial periods. During these earlier times, these basins contained lakes, several of which formed a continuous chain, draining north through the Amargosa Desert to the Amargosa River and ultimately to Death Valley. It is not clear if Mesquite Valley was a part of this system (Morrison 1965).

C. Central Hills and Tecopa Basin (Middle Amargosa) Sub-Area

At Eagle Mountain, the Amargosa River drops below 600 meters in elevation and runs roughly south for about 33 kilometers, meandering within the confines of gravel bluffs formed by alluvial fans from the Greenwater Range to the west, and the Resting Springs Range to the east. Near the southern end of the Greenwater Range are the Dublin Hills (maximum elevation 926 meters), located directly west of the village of Shoshone, where the valley of the Amargosa broadens out and merges into the Tecopa Basin. The Tecopa Basin lies generally below 600 meters elevation, dropping below 400 meters above sea level near Tecopa, where the Amargosa River has cut a gorge through the Sperry and Alexander Hills in its course south. Tecopa Basin is bound on the west by Ibex Hills, which have crestlines roughly between 1000 and 1250 meters above sea level. To the southeast are the Alexander Hills, with slightly higher elevations (over 790 meters). These lower hills are composed of sedimentary formations of late Tertiary and earlier Quarternary age, except along their northeastern margin, where formations geologically similar to the Nopah and Resting Springs

Ranges are found.

The Tecopa Basin proper has extensive lacustrine sediments of perhaps mid-Pleistocene age, which have been heavily eroded and partially replaced by sediments from the Amargosa River. Northwest of Shoshone, Tecopa Basin merges into the lower Greenwater Valley, and on the southeast merges into Chicago Valley. Emigrant Pass provides easy access between Tecopa Basin and California Valley.

D. Southern Uplands Sub-Area

The eastern boundary of this sub-area is formed by the Clark Mountain Range and the Mesquite Mountains, which merge into the Kingston Range. Alexander Hills and Sperry Hills lie to the north. This southwestern portion of the study area contains Shadow Valley, and the Kingston Wash drainage system. Shadow Valley (and Kingston Wash) extends south of Valley Wells at I-15, toward Cima Dome, outside the study area. Shadow Valley is a broad, enclosed alluvial basin, merging, on the east, into the Shadow Mountains and Squaw Mountain. At Valley Wells, Shadow Valley lies approximately 1100 meters above sea level, with the valley floor sloping down to the north to an elevation of about 900 meters at the point where Kingston Wash cuts west through the foothills between the Kingston Range (on the north) and the Shadow Mountains (on the south). Kingston Wash has cut a shallow gorge for a distance of about 18 kilometers trending west and emerging into Valjean Valley, at which point the elevation of the wash is about 600 meters. South of the Kingston Wash gorge, roughly 19 kilometers east-west by 29 kilometers north-south, lies a general upland area with rather varied relief. The northern half of this area is occupied by the Shadow Mountains, lying generally between 900 and 1200 meters above sea level. These formations consist of earlier pre-Cambrian granitic and metamorphic rocks and Tertiary sedimentary rocks. Erosion has been extensive here, leaving a maze of isolated ridges, hills and mesas, sometimes steep and rugged, and containing features such as arches, holes-in-the-wall and numerous shelters and grottos. Drainage in the Shadow Mountains is generally north or west toward Kingston Wash. South of Shadow Mountain is a similar but somewhat higher series of upland features. On the east, abutting Shadow Valley, is an isolated series of hills around Squaw Mountain which, at an elevation of 1488 meters, is the highest point in the Southern Uplands sub-area. West of Squaw Mountain is the Turquoise Mountain area, with elevations to slightly over 1200 meters above sea level. Southwest of Turquoise Mountain are the Hollow Hills, with crestline elevations up to 1150 meters. North of the Shadow Hills are the Silurian Hills (largely outside the study area), at the southern edge of Valjean Valley, which have several peaks and crestlines 900 meters above sea level.

The remaining area includes a small portion of the northeastern section of the Avawatz Mountains, the outlying Salt

Spring Hills, and the lower course of the Amargosa River as it emerges from Sperry Hills, joins Salt Creek and flows westward into the southern end of Death Valley. This is the lowest part of the project area, lying from 600 meters to less than 80 meters above sea level. Although much higher elevations are attained, the portion of the Avawatz Mountains included in the study area generally does not exceed 900 meters above sea level. The Salt Spring Hills are low lying but fairly rugged and rise to about 500 meters. Noteworthy in this sector are the Dumont Sand Dunes, northwest and east of Salt Spring Hills in an area about 16 by 3 kilometers. These feature most dune types including star and whale back dunes, rising to as much as 120 meters above the surrounding ground level, in the central area, barchan or crescentic dunes along the eastern edge near Valjean Hills, and transverse or longitudinal dunes along the southern margin. Although they are not considered to be migrating dunes, the Valjean Hills to the east exhibit a partial mantle of sand (MacDonald 1970).

The remainder of this sub-area lies mostly within the drainage of Kingston Wash, except for the western and southern portions of the Hollow Hills and Turquoise Mountain, which have drainage directly into Silver Lake (outside the study area) and Salt Creek. The westernmost portion of the Kingston Wash system is Valjean Valley, north of, but not including, Silurian Lake. Valjean Valley is entirely below 600 meters above sea level, except for Valjean Hills, in the northeast and near the lower foothills of the Kingston Range. These low, but rugged hills rise to a maximum elevation of 670 meters above sea level. Valjean Valley slopes west, dropping to about 150 meters above sea level, on the east side of the Salt Spring Hills, near the confluence of Kingston Wash and Salt Creek.

E.   The Southeastern Massifs and Ivanpah Valley Sub-Area

The southeastern section of the project area includes the highest and most rugged uplands area. This high country includes: the Kingston Range, south of Pahrump Valley and north of Shadow Valley; the Mesquite Mountains, diagonally southeast of Kingston Range and lying on the west side of Mesquite Lake; and the Clark Mountain Range, which forms a partial arc north and west of Ivanpah Valley.

The Kingston Range rises rather abruptly above the surrounding areas, to form a high central area roughly 12 by 16 kilometers in extent, of steep canyons, ridges and high meadows ranging in elevation from 1200 meters above sea level to Kingston Peak, at 2232 meters. The Mesquite Mountains are separated from the Kingston Range by a broad pass area lying slightly below 1100 meters above sea level. Upper elevations in the Mesquite Mountains exceed 1200 meters above sea level, to a maximum of 1572 meters. The Clark Mountain Range is a rugged, compact upland area mostly above 1200 meters elevation, with the highest elevation at Clark

Mountain, 2416 meters above sea level. Ivanpah Valley, which constitutes the southeasternmost portion of the study area, is an area of internal drainage approximately 40 kilometers long. The section of Ivanpah Valley which lies within the project area is west of Interstate 15 and the California-Nevada state boundary, and includes alluvial outwash from the Clark Mountain Range on the west, and the northern portion of Ivanpah Lake, a playa basin at 793 meters above sea level.

Geologically, this sub-area is no less complex than others, and has similar formations, particularly the later pre-Cambrian and Paleozoic sedimentary rocks noted previously for the Nopah and Resting Springs Ranges. These formations continue south along the northeastern portion of the Kingston Range, and down into the Mesquite Mountains and the Clark Mountain Range. The southwestern portion of the Kingston Range is principally Mesozoic-Tertiary granitic rocks. Volcanics occur but are less common than in the Greenwater Range, for example. Ivanpah Valley appears to be the result of extensive faulting and warping.

Climate

The climate of the project area is characterized by low rainfall, high evaporation rates, broad diurnal temperature ranges (which are fairly consistent in terms of maxima, minima and mean values), and periodically strong seasonal winds. The greatest variations within these patterns relate to elevation, the "rain-shadow" effect of the Sierra Nevada and Panamint Ranges west of the project area, and, of course, the season of the year. Rainfall comes mainly in the winter months from December to March, and in the summer months from July to September. The average annual rainfall ranges from about three inches in lower, sheltered elevations to over eight inches in areas of higher elevation. Extremes may vary from virtually no measurable rainfall to over fifteen inches in any one year. A specific locality may receive no measurable rainfall for several years, then receive more rain in one incredibly-intense episode (lasting only a few hours) than its annual average. Perhaps the most noteworthy features of rainfall in the Northeast Mojave are that it is low and quite unpredictable.

Mean temperatures range from about 40°F in January to around 90°F in July. Extreme low temperatures average near 0°F, with extreme high temperatures around 120°F. These values vary with elevation, low valleys are generally hotter and mountains cooler.

Biotic Zones and Communities

The discussion of the biotic background of the project area has been generated from several sources. Bradley and Deacon (1967), for example, have classified and described the biotic communities of Clark County, Nevada, which is immediately east of the project area. Although Clark County is larger and more diversified than

the study area, the two hold much in common. Other sources
consulted were Munz and Keck (1968), Jaeger (1941 and 1957),
Munz (1962), Benson (1957) and Jaeger and Smith (1971). Much
of the information presented here is the result of five months
of field work in the project area, during which one task of the
field team was to identify plants and animals associated with
the Inventory units. Field observations were limited, of course,
by the season (November,1977 to March, 1978), and by the difficulty of identifying birds and reptiles under normal field circumstances. Field identification of common plants was considerably enhanced by consultations with Eric Ritter of the BLM Desert
Planning Staff, and Joseph King, ethnobotanist with the University
of Nevada, Las Vegas, who willingly shared their knowledge of
East Mojave flora. The following discussion is concerned with
floral communities primarily; faunal observations will be summar-
ized at the end of this section.

In any arid or semi-arid section of the earth, plant and
animal distributions are primarily dependent on a combination of
circumstances. The most significant factors in these natural
distributions are elevation, temperature ranges, rainfall, soils
and groundwater conditions. All of these factors are taken into
account in the following discussion.

A. Creosote - Burrobush Community

The Creosote-Burrobush community is by far the most widespread plant association within the project area. The dominant
species are the creosote bush (Larrea sp.) and burrobush (Ambrosia
sp.), either of which may occur in virtually pure stands. This
community occurs from about 150 meters to 1500 meters above sea
level. It is most commonly found on valley floors, adjacent
bajadas and alluvial fans. Soils are commonly a gray, desert soil
derived from alluvial deposits, and usually have a high content of
salts, particularly calcium carbonate. A caliche layer is commonly present, being particularly noticeable when exposed along washes
in sloping terrain. The so-called "desert pavement" phenomenon
is fairly common, particularly on the bajadas associated with the
eastern slopes of the Greenwater Range; in other localities desert
pavement may occur on interfluves near the tops of outwash areas.
Generally these patches of desert pavement have less than 1% plant
coverage.

Other most common constituents of the Creosote-Burrobush community are: Yucca, particularly Y. shidigera (the Mojave yucca);
cacti, particularly Opuntia sp., Echinocereus sp., Echinocactus
sp. and Mamillaria sp.; spiny herb (Chorizanthe sp.); buckwheat
(Eriogonum sp.); loco weed (Astragalus sp.); various saltbush
or scale plants (Atriplex sp.); Mormon tea (Ephedra sp.); thorn
bushes (Lycium sp.); chia (Salvia sp.); brittle-bush (Encelia sp.);
goldenbush (Haplopappus sp.); spiny hopsage (Grayia spinosa),
winter fat (Eurotia sp.), desert lily (Hesperocallis undulata),
and desert sunflower (Geraea sp.) As this list could go on

-11-

some length, it is perhaps sufficient to say that there is considerable variation in plant species within the Creosote-Burrobush community. The percentage of plant coverage is variable, probably resulting directly from the amount of ground water available; most localities have between 10 and 20%. Some areas have very sparse cover, particularly Valjean Valley north of Kingston Wash. This bleak landscape can be transformed, however, by the advent of heavy rainfall (such as occurred in December 1977 through March 1978 resulting in the appearance of millions of small annual flowering plants). A particularly spectacular sight brought on by the winter rains is the desert sunflower (Geraea canescens), occurring in sandy wash and hill areas below 900 meters.

Within the Creosote-Burrobush community are found several variant patterns related to certain local conditions, particularly drainage; some of these variants, are trans-zonal, such as Desert Wash and Stream Riparian communities, and are discussed below, others are enclaves or mosaic patterns within the broader Creosote-Burrobush community.

B. Blackbrush Community

Within the upper limits of the Creosote-Burrobush community, a single species, Coleogyne ramosissima or blackbrush, occurs with increasing frequency and may even entirely replace the Creosote-Burrobush community at elevations over 900-1000 meters. Individual plants of Coleogyne may also occur as a minor Creosote-Burrobush community constituent as low as 600 meters. The Joshua tree (Yucca brevifolia) is often found in association with Coleogyne belts. Other common plant associations are Mojave yucca (Y. schidigera), banana yucca (Y. baccata), creosote, Mormon tea (Ephedra sp.), spiny hopsage (Grayia spinosa), winter fat (Eurotia lanata), goldenbush (Haplopappus sp.), brittlebush (Encelia farinosa), and thornbush (Lycium sp.). Other plant associates of the Blackbrush community zones, but with limited ranges, are: Parry's nolina (Nolina parryi wolfii), found only on upper ridges and meadows at elevations of 1200 to 1500 meters above sea level in the Kingston Range; and agave (Agave utahensis nevadensis), found in great numbers in association with limestone formations on the eastern and southern flanks of the Clark Mountain Range, at elevations from 1200 to 1600 meters above sea level. Scattered through the upper margins of the Blackbrush belt, scrub juniper (Juniperus osteosperma) may also occur at elevations above 1200 meters in the Clark Mountain and Kingston Range. Juniper, as a stunted relic, was also observed in a few localities in the eastern flanks of the Greenwater Range. It is likely that juniper and its frequent associate, piñon pine, were once much more widespread at lower elevations, during moister climatic regimes which have prevailed in the past (cf. Mehringer 1967).

Soil in the Blackbrush community is developed from older alluvium and is of the gray desert type, with higher organic content and lower salt concentrations than at lower elevations.

The Blackbrush community is widespread within the study area and is found along the upper bajadas and lower flanks of all the mountain ranges and hilly upland areas.

C. Desert Wash Community

Large dry water courses, which pass through both the Blackbrush and the Creosote-Burrobush communities, often have a distinctive plant assemblage. Here certain species, which occur only incidentally in the surrounding communities, are much more common. The dominant plants in this community are low shrubs such as cheesebush (Hymenoclea sp.), several species of buckwheat (Eriogonum sp.), goldenbush (Haplopappus sp.), Mormon tea (Ephedra sp.), thorn bush (Lycium sp.), winter fat (Eurotia sp.), trees such as cat claw (Acacia sp.), mesquite (Prosopis sp.), desert willow (Chilopsis sp.), desert mistletoe (Phoradendron sp.) and occasionally salt cedar (Tamarix sp. [an introduced plant]), and various grasses, especially bunch grass (Stipa sp.). Soils are usually silty to sandy but may be rather gravelly and rocky, especially at higher elevations. This type of community is common in the study area, particularly in the large alluvial fans emanating from the higher mountain ranges. For the most part, the Desert Wash community is not particularly conspicuous. Several water courses, however, have a much heavier growth of trees, particularly mesquite, willow (Salix sp.) and salt cedar. This is a localized but extensive phenomenon, particularly along Salt Creek from the confluence with Kingston Wash to Salt Springs, intermittently along the Amargosa River in Tecopa Basin, and along the Amargosa River near the northern end of the study area. In the last case, a dense impenetrable thicket of mesquite and other trees exists as a continuous swath along the course of the normally dry river bed for 9 or 10 kilometers. This grove continues some distance south toward Death Valley Junction in attenuated form, where it becomes scattered, open and intermittent.

The upper reaches of washes and adjacent cliffs and steep-walled canyons at elevations above 1500 meters in the Clark Mountain and Kingston Range. also frequently have a somewhat different plant assemblage from the surrounding blackbrush or piñon-juniper zones. Common in this context are taller shrubs and woody plants such as cliff rose (Cowania sp.), Apache plume (Fallugia sp.), rabbitbrush (Chrysothamnus sp.), squawbush (Rhus sp.), desert almond (Prunus fasiculata), barberry (Barberis sp.), Yucca sp., Agave sp., service berry (Amelanchier sp.), manzanita (Arctostaphylos sp.), ash (Fraxinus sp.), and mountain mahogany (Cercocarpus sp.).

D. Playa or Alkalai Sink Community

Dry or ephemeral lake beds are found in Ivanpah, Mesquite, Pahrump and Stewart valleys, in the Tecopa Basin, and in the Amargosa Desert directly north of Eagle Mountain. Old lake sediments are also present at Valley Wells in Shadow Valley, north-

west of Valjean Valley near Dumont Dunes, at the south end of
California Valley east of Tecopa Pass, and at the southern end
of Death Valley. Although these latter are not basins, they
all share with the true basins certain characteristic floral
assemblages and distributions.

The actual lake beds are barren, covered with silts and
sometimes heavily encrusted with salts. Beyond the margins of
the salt-pan proper are various salt tolerant plants, particularly inkweed (Suaeda torreyana), pickleweed (Allenrolfea occi-
dentalis), various species of Atriplex, particularly shadscale
(A. confertifolia) and desert holly (A. hymenelytra). Also
frequently present are hopsage (Grayia spinosa) and winter fat
(Eurotia lanata). This assemblage may vary from one part of the
playa margin to another, and differs between playas. At Ivanpah
Lake it is attenuated, with some Atriplex sp. and hopsage merging
with the creosote community a few meters from the barren playa
margin. The plant community is well developed at Mesquite Lake,
where the pickleweed-inkweed belt gives way to an assemblage of
mesquite, willow, cat-claw, grasses, scattered Atriplex sp. and
creosote. This belt, dominated by an extensive mesquite grove,
completely encircles Mesquite Lake. On the eastern side of Mesquite Lake is an extensive area of sand dunes, usually capped
with mesquite and cat-claw. Scattered mesquite, marginal to the
open playas, are also present at Pahrump and Stewart Valley,
Tecopa Basin and at Ash Meadows (Amargosa Desert).

E. Springside Community

Springs in the project area are widely scattered, with a
tendency to be more concentrated in certain localities, such as
Tecopa Basin and the Kingston Range, and almost totally lacking
in others, such as Valjean and Shadow valleys. Most of the
springs in the project area are now inactive, but the remainder
support a distinctive floral assemblage. Among the latter are
Chappo and Resting Springs in Tecopa Basin, Twelve Mile Spring
in Chicago Valley, and Salt Spring west of Valjean Valley. Other
springs such as Bull Springs near Turquoise Mountain, Owl Hole
Springs, Ivanpah Springs, and Tule Spring (California Valley)
are either inactive or have been drastically altered by stockmen
and miners in the historic period. Plant species commonly associated with these springs are sedges (Carex sp., Scirpus sp.),
rush (Juncus sp.), cattails (Typha sp.), trees such as willow
(Salix sp.), cottonwood (Populus sp.), mesquite (Prosopis sp.)
and the introduced salt cedar (Tamarix sp.). Also present are
grasses and several salt tolerant Chenopodiaceae (Atriplex sp.,
etc.).

F. Sand Dunes

Dumont Dunes, northwest and east of Salt Spring Hills, is
the only extensive dune system in the project area. Information
from other sand dune areas in the Mojave Desert suggests that

there is a reasonable expectation that plants seasonally present
in dune swales, blowout pockets and along dune borders would
include rice grass (Oryzopsis hymenoides), panic grass (Panicum
sp.), wild rhubarb (Rumex sp.), Spanish needle (Palafoxia linearis),
primrose (Oenothera sp.) and perhaps one or more species of wild
buckwheat (Eriogonum sp.). The project had several sample units
near these dunes, but at the wrong time of year to confirm or
deny the presence of these plants. Confirmation of the presence
of rice grass would be an interesting factor in the evaluation of
the series of aboriginal sites recorded by M.J. Rogers and others
(C.N. Warren, personal communication) at Salt Springs and along
the west side of Dumont Dunes and along the nearby Amargosa River.

G. Piñon-Juniper Community

At elevations above 1500 meters in the Kingston and Clark
Mountain ranges, an open woodland occurs in which piñon (Pinus
monophylla) and juniper (Juniperus sp.) are the most frequent
and conspicuous elements. These woodlands are open, in that the
trees are dispersed, giving a park-like appearance. Other plants
which may occur as understory or in widely scattered association
are oak (Quercus sp.), ash (Fraxinus sp.), barberry (Berberis sp.),
Manzanita (Arctostaphylos sp.), service berry (Amelanchier sp.),
gooseberry (Ribes sp.), mountain mahogany (Cercocarpus sp.) and
mistletoe (Phoradendron sp.). Soil in the Piñon-Juniper woodland is generally a sandy loam, well-drained, light brown in
color, with some development of distinct soil profiles and a
higher organic content than soils at lower elevations.

Although the Piñon-Juniper community occurs in only two
localities and constitutes a very small part of the total project
area, it was an important resource area for the foraging peoples
who occupied this territory prior to the intrusion of bearers of
European-derived cultures.

H. Riparian Community

At present there is only one locality which has a permanent
or semi-permanent flowing stream. This is the Amargosa River at
Tecopa which flows for some distance southward into the river gorge
through Sperry Hills. The presence of a regular water supply
supports an intermittent Riparian plant community along the
benches and banks adjacent to the river, and for a short distance
along the canyon at China Ranch, which is a tributary to the Amargosa. Vegetation occurs in dense thickets and includes mesquite
(Prosopis sp.), willow (Salix sp.), cottonwood (Populus sp.),
salt cedar (Tamarix gallica), arrowweed (Pluchea sp.), goosefoot
(Chenopodium sp.), sedges (Carax sp.), rushes (Juncus sp.), and
cattails (Typha sp.). Introduced palm and tamarix trees were
also observed by the field team at China Ranch.

I. Faunal Observations

Observations of fauna in the study area were severely restricted by the season, by the difficulty of identifying certain fauna without collecting, and by the limited expertise of the field team. Some sightings, particularly of small lizards and songbirds were so fleeting that no attempt could be made for any more than a very generalized notation. Some species of animals tend to have a very limited range or territory and may be specific to certain plant communities (or biotic zones), while others are too limited to attempt any such segregation of the data, or to attempt to compare them with listings from the scientific literature.

The following constitutes a comprehensive list of fauna observed during the course of the fieldwork:

1. Invertebrates
    Orb web spider
    Funnel web spider
    Tarantula
    Flies
    Ants
    Grasshoppers
    Wingless wasp (Velvet Ant)
    Bees, Wasps
    Butterflies
    Moths
    Beetles

2. Reptiles
    Various small lizards including:
        Desert Iguana (Dipsosaurus sp.)
        Spiny Lizard (Sceloporus sp.)
        Desert Horned Lizard (Phrynosoma sp.)
    Desert Tortoise (Gopherus agassizi), bones and carapace
    Snakes, non-poisonous

3. Birds
    Hawks or Falcons
    Owls
    Warblers
    Finch
    Meadowlark
    Numerous small song birds
    Waterfowl (Grimshaw Lake, Tecopa)
    Great Blue Heron (Grimshaw Lake, Tecopa)
    Quail
    Roadrunner (Geococcyx sp.)
    Raven or Crow (Corvus sp.)

4. Mammals
   Bat, guano
   Wood Rat (Neotoma sp.), nests
   Spermophilus sp. and other small rodents
   Badger
   Blacktail Jackrabbit (Lepus californicus)
   Desert Cottontail (Sylvilagus sp.)
   Coyote (Canis latrans)
   Desert Bighorn (Ovis canadensis)
   Wild burro (feral, introduced)
   Wild horse (feral, introduced)

CHAPTER 3. CULTURAL/HISTORICAL REVIEW

Robert H. Crabtee and Elizabeth Warren

Assisted by Tara Shepperson

This chapter presents a brief review of the prehistory and history of the Northeast Mojave region. The purpose of this review is to provide the reader with sufficient background material to be able to place the present work in proper perspective and to permit an intelligent reading of this report, in its entirety. A much more detailed overview of the archaeology and history of the project area is presently being prepared, under separate contract, by Dr. Claude N. Warren of the University of Nevada, Las Vegas.

A. The Prehistoric Period

Archaeological surveys within the project area have been conducted by M.J. Rogers, William J. Wallace, Alice and Charles Hunt, James Benton, and others. Excavation has been minimal, and the results, so far, presented in only preliminary form (McKinney et al. 1971; Knight 1973; Gearhart 1974). Although no local chronology has been established, a general chronological framework has been suggested for the Mojave Desert by various investigators (Rogers 1945; Hunt 1960; Wallace 1962). This has been modified as more data have become available and dating made more precise. Two recent papers place these data in a temporal framework, buttressed with radiocarbon dates. One chronological scheme, offered by Warren and Crabtree (in press), pertains specifically to the Mojave Desert. Hester (1973) has presented a more general scheme relevant to the Great Basin, which complements the Warren-Crabtree chronology. Together, these frameworks suggest the following interpretations:

1. Period I (10,000 B.C. to 5,000 B.C.)

The Early Western Pluvial Lakes (or Lake Mojave) Tradition appears to consist of two well-defined assemblages, the San Dieguito and the Haskomat. A third possible assemblage consists only of fluted points which occur occasionally as isolated surface finds in the Eastern Mojave Desert and Western Nevada. The latter are stylistically and technologically similar to the Clovis and Folsom points of the Southwest, but are undated and associations with the other two complexes have not been determined.

The San Dieguito complex is perhaps best known from the C.W. Harris sites (Warren and True 1961) in San Diego County, California. This complex is widespread in the Southern California deserts and the western Great Basin (Campbell et al. 1937); Rogers 1939 and 1966; Brainerd 1953; Heizer 1965; Warren and Ranere 1968; Warren 1967 and 1970), and after some controversy now seems well established. Adjacent to the study area, it has been indentified at Soda and Silver playas (Pleistocene Lake Mojave) and in Death Valley (Hunt 1960). The San Dieguito complex is characterized by a crude stone flaking technology, particularly evident on leaf-shaped biface points and knives, and several types of distinctive domed scrapers. This flaking technology is identified by irregular edges, deep bulbs of percussion and step fractures, irregular surfaces, and flat crushed edges suggesting an anvil support. At the C.W. Harris Site, the San Dieguito complex has been dated from somewhat before 7080 B.C. to 6000 B.C.

The Haskomat complex (8000 B.C. to 5000 B.C.) has some stylistic similarities with the San Dieguito complex but differs from it technologically. Distinctive artifact types include points with sloping shoulders and long parallel-sided stems, sometimes called "Haskett points." Mojave points, and possibly Silver Lake points, from the Mojave Desert in Southern California and Southern Nevada may be variant types or part of a closely related complex. Other artifact types included in the Haskomat complex are crescents, spoke shaves and gravers of characteristic types. Less distinctive are scrapers, leaf-shaped points and knives (Warren and Ranere 1968).

Haskomat is present at Lake Mojave and has been identified in several localities in Central and Southern Nevada. It is most widespread in the northwestern Great Basin in Nevada, Oregon and Idaho, and often found at surface sites along old shorelines of Pleistocene lakes. Haskomat does appear to be of northern origin, perhaps occurring as far north as Lind Coulee in the channeled scabland section of Central Washington. This complex has been given an estimated date range of 8000 to 5000 B.C., but may be older.

Deposits dated at 10,000-13,000 years with associated artifacts, are known from Tule Springs near Las Vegas, Nevada. However, this collection of material is so small and generalized, or otherwise nondescript, that a summary of distinctive material cannot be offered at this time (Shutler 1967).

The economic pose of this period is thought to have been basically a lakeside adaptation, during a period of wetter and slightly cooler climate in contrast to today.

A chronological gap of around 2000 years between 600 and 4000 B.C. in the Mojave Desert is probably more apparent than real and may reflect the status of research in the region, generally, rather than a depopulation related to progressive dessication of the desert following the termination of the last glaciation. We have chosen to divide this apparent gap in half and incorporate it into Periods I and II as defined here. Continued research should eventually clarify this problematical period.

2. Period II (5000 B.C. to 2000 B.C.)

A series of projectile (dart) point styles serve, rather shakily, as the diagnostic elements for the period from 5000 to 2000 B.C.. These include Silver Lake points, the Humboldt series and the Pinto series. The latter is a very widespread style and has turned up from coastal Southern California to Idaho, but is most frequently found in Central Nevada and the Mojave Desert. The Humboldt series is also widespread, but is best documented in the northern Great Basin. The Silver Lake style of point, also widespread in Southern California and Nevada, is much more ambiguous as a type (or series of closely related types) and is also chronologically problematic. Silver Lake points have not been found in dated associations, but have turned up in many localities in the Mojave Desert, as surface material with several other varieties of Mojave points (Campbell and Campbell 1935; Campbell et al. 1937; Rogers 1939; Harrington 1957; Hunt 1960; Susia 1964; Worman 1969; for a brief discussion, see also Hester 1973: 23-45). Lacking a stratigraphic context (except Harrington 1957), no firm dates can be assigned to these occurrences.

Dates from the northern Great Basin for the Humboldt series range from 3920 to 1100 B.C. and, for the Pinto series, from 3350 to 670 B.C. (Hester 1973). At the Stahl Site, near Little Lake, the most characteristic artifact associations of Pinto-Humboldt-Silver Lake and Mojave points are leaf-shaped points and knives, several varieties of well-made scrapers, including elongate keeled scrapers, distinctive flake scrapers, large scraper planes, drills, gravers and milling stones (mano and metate and, occasionally, mortars and pestles; Harrington 1957).

Unfortunately the excavation techniques and analytical premises and procedures which led to these findings were not as carefully implemented as we have come to expect of more recent investigations, but this work was conducted at a time when more refined approaches to ecological, spatial and technological analysis were largely undeveloped. It is clear, for example, that the question of differentiating and refining conceptions of dart point styles for this period remains unanswered. Perhaps as more sophisticated research is undertaken, some of these problems will be resolved.

3. Period III (2000 B.C. to A.D. 500)

Period III is characterized by medium to large-sized stemmed and notched points. Common forms include the Elko series (dated in the Mojave Desert between 1990 B.C. and A.D. 1080; Hester 1973), Humboldt concave-base points and Gypsum Cave points. Assays have been done on material from several sites in the Mojave Desert. Newberry Cave near Barstow yielded one date (on a twig figurine) of 1020 ($\pm$ 250) B.C. (Smith et al. 1957; Smith 1963; Hubbs et al. 1965): Gypsum and Elko series points were found in association. The Rose Springs Site (Lanning 1963), in the southern Owens Valley, gave dates on

five samples ranging from 1950 to 290 B.C.. Of these a date
of 950 B.C. is relevant to the Early Rose Springs component,
and the 290 B.C. date relates to the Middle Rose Springs component (Clewlow et al. 1970). The three earlier dates are
from the lower midden at Rose Springs, which lacks distinctive
or diagnostic artifacts. Early Rose Springs contains Humboldt,
Elko and Gypsum points; Middle Rose Springs has Elko and Gypsum
points, and witnesses the first appearance of the smaller Rose
Springs series points. The Willow Beach Site, on the Colorado
River in Arizona near Boulder Dam, has a date of 250 B.C. on
the Price Butte Phase, which has large points similar to the
Elko series (Schroeder 1961). Gypsum Cave near Las Vegas has
two dates, 450 ($\pm$ 60) B.C. (UCLA 1069) and 950 ($\pm$80) B.C.
(UCLA 1223), applicable to the early Gypsum point-bearing component (Heizer and Berger 1970).

At Stuart Rock shelter in the Eastern Mojave (in Meadow
Valley Wash, Nevada), the earliest levels are dated by radiocarbon at 1920 ($\pm$250) B.C.. This level has points identified
as "Pinto shoulderless" - now called Humboldt concave-base
points. Higher levels contain Elko points and what is probably
a Rose Springs corner-notched point (Shutler et al. 1960).

The Humboldt and Elko series and Gypsum Cave points appear
to represent an overlapping sequence of point types. Humboldt
points appear prior to 2000 B.C., lasting into the earlier
part of the first millenium B.C., Gypsum Cave points occur
between 1000 B.C. and A.D. 1, while Elko points overlap these
two and persist as late as ca. A.D. 500. In the latter part of
this period, there is a diminution of size for Gypsum Cave
points and the Elko series, and about A.D. 500 they are replaced by the Rose Springs-Eastgate series. This reduction
from large dart points to small points is correlated with the
replacement of the atlatl by the bow and arrow.

In summary, this period is characterized by medium to
large dart points of the Humboldt and Elko series, and the
Gypsum Cave points. The millingstone and mano are found generally in the Mojave Desert, but not in large numbers. A variety
of knives, scrapers, drills and other small stone tools are
present, as are stone and shell beads. Other diagnostic traits
include the introduction of incised and painted pebbles and
slate tablets, and the presence of split-twig figurines and
petroglyphs of animals in associations that have been suggested
to be indicative of magic ritual associated with hunting (Schwartz
et al. 1958; Smith et al. 1957; Grant et al. 1968; Hillebrand
1972). In the latter part of this period, small projectile
points replace large points, but retain essentially similar
forms, reflecting the shift from atlatl (dart and throwing
stick) or spear, to bow and arrow.

4. Period IV (ca. A.D. 500 to A.D. 1100)

In the Mojave Desert, west of Cronese Basin and south of

Providence Mountains, Period IV is essentially a continuation of the previous period. The Rose Spring-Eastgate series, slightly smaller than previously, continue with the addition of Cottonwood triangular points in the latter part of the period. Also present is the milling complex (mano, metate, mortar, pestle) as well as incised stones and slate pendants. On the east, and as far north as Death Valley and Ash Meadows (near the study area), there was increased influence and sporadic occupation by Anasazi (Basketmaker III, Pueblo I and II) groups. Permanent Anasazi settlements, including pre-ceramic Basketmaker II, were present in the Muddy-Virgin River area of southeastern Nevada and adjacent southwestern Utah. Although these Virgin Branch Anasazi were primarily sedentary, horticultural folk (Shutler 1961), there is widespread evidence of intermittent forays into southwestern Nevada and adjacent California (Rogers 1939; Hunt 1960; Shutler and Shutler 1962; Worman 1969; Crabtree et al. 1970). Characteristic of the assemblage are Virgin Branch ceramics (gray-wares), shell beads and ornaments, derived from the Pacific and Gulf of California coasts, unbaked clay figurines and miniature carrying baskets, conical pottery pipes and, occasionally in the Turquoise District near Halloran Springs, mauls, picks and turquoise chips. These widespread phenomena probably represent periodic foraging parties, trading excursions to the Pacific coast and turquoise mining parties from the Virgin Branch area.

Sometime during the 12th century A.D., the Anasazi Virgin Branch was abandoned, for as yet unknown reasons, and subsequent developments in the Mojave Desert are attributed to groups still in residence (or nearby) in later, historic times.

5. Period V. (ca. A.D. 1100 to A.D. 1900)

The final period begins with the arrival of Numic (Paiute-Shoshone) peoples, and the departure of the Virgin Branch Anasazi. The causes and processes involved in these population shifts are highly conjectural at present; the problem being the sequence of Numic expansion and Anasazi departure in the Mojave east of Cronese Basin.

Characteristic ceramics of this period are Shoshonean (Owens Valley) or Paiute utility brown-wares, generally found north of the Providence Mountains, and Lower Colorado buff-ware and Tizon brown-wares to the south. Projectile point series are dominated by Desert side-notched and Cottonwood triangular points, although the Rose Springs-Eastgate series continues in reduced numbers in the western part of the Mojave Desert. Several varieties of well-made knives occur, as do drills, gravers, small flake knives and scrapers, manos, metates, pestles, bed-rock and/ or portable mortars, olivella shell beads of several types, bone beads, pendants and occasional pointed tools, incised stones, slate pendants and baked and unbaked clay figurines. Several site varieties have been noted, including roasting pits, "fire" middens, rock shelters, caves and rock alignments.

During the latter part of this period, but prior to the European intrusion into the Mojave Desert region (late 1700's), a branch of the Yuman speaking Mohave Indians began to abandon the Big Maria Mountains. This area was then occupied by groups of Southern Paiutes from the Las Vegas area. This was probably a rather gradual process and reached its greatest extent in the latter half of the 19th Century, before the Reservation Period. The causes for this shift probably related to various wars and population changes, known to have occurred during the 17th and 18th Centuries, in which the Mohave and their allies were ultimately victorious. The ability of the Southern Paiute, or Cheme-huevi as they became known, to take advantage of and exploit this opportunity is a matter which needs to be investigated, and could very well throw some light on earlier Numic movements and adaptive strategies during this final prehistoric period.

6. Summary

The chronological ordering of the pre-history of any region the size and complexity of the Mojave Desert involves a certain amount of oversimplification and arbitrary categorizations. In the present instance, the effort is further complicated by poorly-controlled data or its general absence.

In conclusion, the following chronological ordering of the Mojave Desert Pre-History is offered:

a. Early Man: consisting of three somewhat differentiated traditions - Fluted Point Tradition (not dated, but estimated to be 8000 to 10,000 B.C.); the Western Pluvial Lakes Tradition (dating 8000 to 5000 B.C.) including the stylistically similar but technologically separate San Dieguito complex and the Haskomat complex; and an earlier dated occupation with extinct megafaunal associations, but no distinctive cultural associations (dated at Tule Springs, Nevada, between 13,000 and 10,000 B.C.). This period appears to be one in which large game, as well as lakeside exploitative poses were maintained. During the shifting climatic conditions of the terminal Pleistocene, the question of possible cultural-ethnic connections between these traditions remains unresolved.

b. The Great Basin Archaic (early): representing an adaptation to shifting climatic conditions (generally dryer) by foraging folk, with an emphasis on hunting with possibly long distance seasonal shifting; characterized by a lithic assemblage including a sequence of overlapping point styles from Silver Lake, to Humboldt, to Pinto, to Elko and dating from ca. 5000 to 7000 B.C..

c. Great Basin Archaic (late): a continuation of the previous period with a shift through Humboldt, Elko and Gypsum point styles, culminating with the appearance of small points of the Rose Springs-Eastgate series, an indication of a shift from spear and dart (with atlatl) to bow and arrow.

d. Terminal Great Basin Archaic: a continuation of Period III
    and the rise and disappearance of the Virgin Branch Anasazi
    in the Eastern Mojave Desert in the Muddy-Virgin River drain-
    age. The Rose Springs-Eastgate series now predominates.
    Pottery was introduced by the Anasazi who were seasonal fora-
    gers when not farming the Eastern Mojave River valleys. Dated
    between A.D. 500 and 1100, this period ends with the abandon-
    ment of the Muddy-Virgin River area by the Anasazi.

e. The Numic Period or Late Prehistoric: ca A.D. 1100 to 1900.
    This marks the rapid spread of Numic (Uto-Aztecan) speaking
    peoples represented in historic times by the Southern Paiute
    (and Chemehuevi); characterized by Desert side-notched and
    Cottonwood triangular points, brown-ware ceramics in the
    North, Lower Colorado buff-ware and Tizon brown-ware in the
    South.

f. The Historic Period: A.D. 1775 to present (Casebier 1976).
    This final period marks the intrusion of Europeans into the
    area, and subsequent settlement and industrial exploitation.
    This also marks the destruction of native cultures. The
    historic period is the topic of the remainder of this chapter.

B. The Historic Period

The northeast sections of the Mojave Desert has always been one
of the least known portions of the California Desert. The region is
forbidding even to the modern traveller, with extreme heat and stark
landscape unrelieved by the familiar plants of better watered areas.
The plants characteristic of the Mojave Desert are exotic and unbeau-
tiful to the untutored eye, their sharp, often spiny leaves and
bizarre shapes only adding to the generally hostile aspect of this
dramatic desert.

With no major rivers reaching to the sea, this desert heartland
remained long undisturbed by immigrants from other lands. The native
Paiutes, Chemehuevis, Shoshones and Mohaves had the land to themselves
until 1830, when Antonio Armijo's caravan of New Mexican traders pain-
fully wended their way across the bleak terrain, moving from waterhole to waterhole. The trail these sturdy merchants blazed to California was modified by later users to become the northern branch of
the Old Spanish Trail (Warren 1974; Warren and Roske 1978). John C.
Fremont's exploring expedition passed through from west to east in
1844. His vivid description of the bleak terrain, of the massacre
of the Martinez-Fuentes party at Resting Springs in 1844, and of the
severity of the trail and its effect on livestock, served to discour-
age travellers. At the same time, his map of the region encouraged
people to use this southern trail to the gold fields, and traffic
through the Bitterwater and Amargosa Planning Units increased significantly after its publication in 1845 (Fremont 1851; Warren 1974).
Conversion of the pack trail to a wagon road began in 1847, still
further increasing the use of the difficult trail. This "Mormon
Road" proved to be one of the longest- and heaviest-used wagon roads

in the Far West, not to be replaced by fast, convenient rail transportation until the 20th Century.

Through the Bitterwater Planning Unit passed the 1849 Death
Valley Party, actually comprised of people from several separate
groups (Long 1941). The Wade family's escape route took them
through the Amargosa Planning Unit. The unfortunate experience of
these sojourners gave the region a still more frightful reputation,
and for no one was the area yet a destination.

Beginning in 1847, the Mormons broke through a modified version
of the pack trail of the Spanish/Mexican period, making it suitable
for wagons. As freighting took on an increasingly significant role
in the provisioning of Salt Lake City and the Utah communities,
short cuts were devised until a network of crude roads crisscrossed
the region. Mining camps were connected with nearby ranches and
with main routes to the coast. Notable cutoffs are the Kingston,
1853 (Caravalho 1857) and Cox's of the early 1860's (Ingersoll's
Century Annals of San Bernardino County 1904). Both of these routes
also were used by the gold seekers of Potosi, just over the border
in southern Nevada, an active camp between 1861-63. Two rival stage
lines rocketed over this trail to Potosi in April of 1861 (Los Angeles
Star, 4/13/61).

Military expeditions traversed the areas as early as 1844, the
Fremont expedition. The next official traveller to view a portion
of the area was Lt. R.S. Williamson in 1853, surveying for a railroad route. He apparently penetrated as far as Silurian Dry Lake
before returning to Soda Springs and the well-travelled Mojave Trail
(Williamson 1856). He followed the chain of dry lakes from Soda to
Silver to Silurian, and established that the Mojave River was not
a tributary of the Colorado. In 1855, Lt. Sylvester Mowry journeyed
through from Salt Lake to Los Angeles, following the Mormon Road.
His map of the trail showed a route by Kingston Springs as the best
and shortest way (Bailey 1965). Beginning in 1859, with the estab-
lishment of Camp Cady on the Mojave River and Fort Mojave on the
Colorado at Needles, various military excursions penetrated the
region on punitive expedition against Paiutes and on routine patrols.
Following the withdrawal of the troops from these outposts in the
1860's and 70's, the military were not again important in this region
until the 1940's when the Camp Irwin facility was first opened (Casebier 1972).

The monotony of life in mining camps on this rugged frontier
was broken in 1861 with the arrival of Owen's party of boundary
surveyors in the Kingston, Amargosa and Bitterwater units. This
party experimented with using camels, a startling sight in the
Mojave Desert, and many made important observations regarding
minerals, water supply, Indians and travel routes (Whitney 1865).
In 1866, Governor Henry G. Blasdel of Nevada spent a brief time
in the northern Bitterwater unit on his way from Carson City to
Hiko, Nevada (Stretch 1867).

Lt. Bendire explored the region in 1867, travelling north along the "old emigrant (Salt Lake) trail," departing from it at Salt Creek's junction with the Amargosa, and moving northwest into the southern end of Death Valley. He then moved on to the Washington Mining District in the mountainous region at the southwestern edge of Death Valley. Finally he moved westward along a newly broken trail that crossed the Owlshead Planning Unit via Leach Lake and Owls Head Spring to the Owens Valley Road along the eastern foot-hills of the Sierras.

Wheeler's Surveys West of the 100th Meridian crossed the area numerous times. Summaries of these and other expeditions are contained in the Warren and Roske manuscript (1978) on historic trails and wagon roads.

The desert eventually became the province of civilian rather than military scientists. In 1891, the famous Death Valley exped-ition was sent out to investigate the flora and fauna of that region. This expedition, headed by C. Hart Merriam, covered much of these planning units in its travels and provided the best information to date on the oddities of this strange land (Fisher et al. 1893). In 1898, the San Francisco Call sent Gustav Eisen, a prominent natura-list, to investigate reports of ancient Indian mining (cf. report on Eisen in Warren and Roske 1978). Archaeologist M.J. Rogers returned to the same area in 1929 to map the sites and report on the ancient diggings (Rogers 1929). Since that time, many scien-tific investigations have been conducted in the Mojave Desert's remotest regions, work that is continuing today (e.g. Campbell, Hunt, Wallace, Warren).

No one came to stay in this unhospitable desert until the pre-sence of commercially valuable ores was recognized at Salt Springs in 1850. This gold mining operation of the "Amargoza District", the first on the Mojave Desert, would continue sporadically into the twentieth century (Casebier ms., "Notes Pertaining to Salt Springs", 1974). Other prospects enticed miners to form the Wash-ington District in the 1860's in the Bitterwater Planning Unit, and Ivanpah in the 1870's, in the Kingston Planning Unit. Most of the mines were short lived. The region would finally produce signifi-cant revenues and encourage relatively permanent population beginning in the 1880's, with the recovery of borax and talc, still important today. Other products mined from time to time include salt and lime-stone, molybdenum and other rare minerals and rare earths. Precious metals continued to draw their fair share throughout the 20th Century, but as the richest ores were removed, and the prices of gold and silver dwindled while labor costs climbed, most of these mines shut down and have not reopened despite the existence of ores still in the lodes.

The famous 20-mule teams were revived in the 20th Century to bring borax from Shoshone to Daggett (Belden 2/4/57). Eventually, these valiant teamsters would be replaced by the Tonopah and Tide-water Railroad, a road constructed in 1906 especially to bring the borax to market. The T&T, heading north from the Santa Fe line at Ludlow, passed through the Amargosa and Bitterwater Planning Units into Nevada. Towns established along the road included sites today only known as names on a map: Broadwell, Silver Lake, Riggs, Valjean. The small feeder line, the Death Valley Railroad, connected with the T&T at Death Valley Junction, where it took on passengers lured to the valley in winter, part of Pacific Coast Borax Company's resort operations in the late 1920's. The T&T traffic declined in the '30's, and finally went out of business in 1939. The rails were torn up in 1942-43 (Myrick 1963).

Ranching was a spotty activity in this part of the Mojave. Without significant permanent water supplies, cattle grazing required extensive rangeland to support even a moderate sized herd. The most important ranch in the Amargosa and Bitterwater units was the Yates Ranch in the Shadow Mountain area. The earliest cattle brand on this portion of the desert was registered to Yates in 1894 (Smith 1974). Rock Springs Land and Cattle Co., founded in 1874 and disbanded in 1927, was based in the Kingston Planning Unit and extensive cattle herds were placed on the range in the more easterly and southerly portions of the Mojave Desert. Sheep flocks passed through in the 1850's on their way to California (Westergaard, ed. 1923), and in the late 1870's Basque sheepherders began to penetrate these arid territories because of drought in their traditional grazing lands farther west (Douglass and Bilbao 1975). Goats were introduced into the Mesquite Valley area by a French Canadian, Oliver Rose (cf. manuscript census 1870, Nevada). By 1877, he was either replaced or joined by a Miguel Nevares, probably Basque (cf. Minutes of San Bernardino County Board of Supervisors, and delinquent taxes, 1876 and 1877, San Bernardino Weekly Times Supplement).

In the Resting Springs area, Cub Lee, member of a famous family of "desert rats", took up a homestead in the 1870's. Another famous ranch in the area, the so-called "China Ranch", was only established in 1900 (McKinney 1971). In addition to these locally operated ranches, spreads from the Nevada side of the border in Pahrump Valley and Ash Meadows ran their cattle in the northeastern sector of the Bitterwater unit. These ranches operated as early as 1876 in Pahrump Valley (Paher 1971). There are some active BLM leases for grazing still operating in the California-Nevada border area, but the number of animals has greatly diminished as the range has been overgrazed.

The 20th Century saw the advent of the automobile, which has permanently changed the character of the Mojave Desert settlements. Those located along auto routes to serve the motoring public survived when those that served mines or the railroads dwindled and died. The Los Angeles Chamber of Commerce placed road signs in the desert as early as 1908, and the Automobile Club of Southern California began to publish road maps of the desert as far back as 1912. In 1914, the first automobile road was constructed through the desert. It passed through the Kingston and Mojave units originally; in 1927, a shortcut of this "Arrowhead Trail" was constructed that moved the route south to the present I-15 alignment via Baker and through Mountain Pass. Small settlements cluster along the road at strategic stops where automobiles can be serviced, and where water is found. The U.S. Geological Survey Water Supply Papers describing watering holes on the desert were much appreciated by early travellers (cf. Mendanhall 1909; Thompson 1929).

Development of automobile travel brought a new type of traveller to the desert - the recreational user. With increased awareness of the extraordinary natural resource of Death Valley, Congress was pressured into establishing the Death Valley National Monument in 1933. There is new pressure to establish a Mojave National Park in the Eastern Mojave just south of these planning units here discussed. This is in part a reaction to the overuse of the desert by the indiscriminate off-road vehicle driver, whose activities in the "barren" wilderness have caused significant destruction of the resources and whose long range effects have yet to be understood.

Industrial facilities in the form of power transmission lines and telephone cables were introduced into the region in the 1940's and 1950's (Mohahve 1963). Still earlier, telegraph wires linked the small settlements along the rail tracks of the Tonopah and Tidewater to the port cities of California. Today microwave radio, television and telephone transmission discs dot the landscape on high promontories where signals will travel unobstructed.

The presence of the Bureau of Land Management was little felt until recent years, when positive management policies were instituted in place of the earlier, permissive ones. The mandate of Congress for a management plan by the early 1980's has placed an extraordinary emphasis on the gathering of data for this vast area. The concept of the desert as wasteland is changing to the desert as a fragile resource; new management plans are on the horizon and the future is not clear, as all previously permitted activities are being evaluated for their impact on the land.

CHAPTER 4. SAMPLING DESIGN

This chapter outlines the ARID-I sampling design, which involves a 1% (approximate) sample of the project area. The sample consists of 209 sampling units, each unit one mile long and one-eighth mile wide, as required under the contract (see Chapter 1, Section E).

The sample is further divided into two stages, which were implemented chronologically. Stage I contains 140 units, or approximately two/thirds of the total sample; Stage II includes the remaining 69 units.

The Stage I sample is a stratified random sample, based on general environmental categories. The Stage II sample involves a dispersed cluster sample consisting of seven, non-randomly selected, areal "blocks," each containing a systematic sample of from eight to twelve sample units.

A. Sampling Universe

The samples were drawn exclusively from the ARID-I project area as described in Chapter 1, Section B. More specifically, the relevant sampling universe consisted of the above area less all parcels which were not under BLM or State of California jurisdiction at the time of sample selection (For the most part, California State lands consist of sections 16 and 36 of a majority of the townships within the project area; these are undeveloped tracts reserved for State school use).

B. Stage I

The Stage I sample (140 units) was cross-stratified using three general environmental variables: landform, vegetation and water resources. Within each variable, the following categories were distinguished:

1. Landform
   a. Mountain
   b. Valley
   c. Playa

2. Vegetation
   a. Juniper/pinon
   b. Mesquite
   c. Other vegetation

3. Water resources
   a. Amargosa River
   b. Wells and reservoirs
   c. Tanks

d. Springs
e. Other water resources

Each of these three variables was measured using data available on USGS 15' topographic maps, plus additional water resource data provided by the BLM Desert Planning Staff. These data, together with the existing cadastral system, were employed to cross-partition the sampling universe. The procedures used to prepare this cross-partition were as follows:

1. Each cadastral section (usually one square mile in area) was evaluated with respect to each of the three stratifying variables; that is, each section fell into three categories, one category for each of the three variables. Thus, for example, a given section might be classified as "valley/mesquite/other water resource" or as "mountain/other vegetation/spring," and so on.

2. To classify each section with respect to the above system, the following set of operational definitions was employed:
   a. Landform
      1) Playa. If any portion of a given section contained land identified as playa on the topographic maps, that section was classified as "playa."
      2) Mountain, Valley. For sections not classified as "playa," if the change in elevation (using topographic map contour lines) within a section exceeded 600 feet, it was categorized as "mountain;" otherwise it was categorized as "valley." Sections containing mountain/valley interface were classified as either "mountain" or "valley" depending on whether over 50% of the section area fell in the mountain or valley categories (Note: There is one exception to the above sheme. The upper slopes of the Greenwater Mountains, which are mesa-like, have been classified as "mountain," despite the relative absence of elevation change).
   b. Vegetation
      1) Juniper/pinon, Mesquite. All sections containing area which was green-keyed on the topographic maps was categorized as either "juniper/pinon" or "mesquite," depending on elevation.
      2) Other vegetation. All sections not classified as either "juniper/piñon" or "mesquite" received the "other vegetation" classification.
   c. Water resources.
      1) Wells and reservoirs, Tanks, Springs. All sections containing point sources of water (i.e. wells and reservoirs, tanks, springs - using the BLM and topographic map data) were classified accordingly.
      2) Amargosa River. All sections not containing point sources but which are passed through by the Amargosa River (as indicated on the topographic maps) received this classification.

-30-

3) Other water resources. All remaining sections were placed in this category.

By combining variables, each section could thus be assigned to 3 x 3 x 5 = 45 possible cross-partition categories. In actuality, only 18 of the 45 possible categories exist in the sampling universe. These 18 categories, and the number of sections assigned to each, are shown in Table 4-1.

Having cross-classified each section according to the above system, the next step was to obtain a representative sample of sections from each category. First, samples were drawn for poorly-represented categories. In determining sample size, the following criteria were used:

1. If a category was represented by three or fewer sections, all such sections were included in the sample;

2. If a category was represented by 4 to 37 sections, three sections were randomly selected, using a random numbers table;

3. For categories represented by 38 to 100 sections, a 1%+ sample (i.e. the minimum number of sections required to provide a 1% sample) was randomly selected, again using a table of random numbers.

The above procedures exhausted all cross-partition categories, with the exception of "mountain/other vegetation/other water resources" and "valley/other vegetation/other water resources." A total of 46 sections had also been selected for the sample. This left 94 sections still to be chosen to complete the Stage I sample. These remaining sections were distributed between the two remaining categories so that the sample proportions (i.e. the number of sections sampled per total number of sections) representing the "mountain" and "valley" were approximately equal. A random numbers table was again used to select sections in these remaining categories.

The number of sections eventually selected from each of the 18 stratification categories is shown in Table 4-2.

Having obtained a stratified sample of sections, it was then necessary to perform a second random draw to locate sampling units within the selected sections. The idealized one-square-mile section was divided into eight vertical zones, each zone one mile long (north-south) and 1/8 mile wide (east-west). Each zone within the section received a number, from 1 to 8, moving from left (west) to right (east). Again using a random numbers table, one zone within each selected section was chosen. These 140 zones served as the sampling units inventoried during the Stage I fieldwork. The locations of each are roughly mapped by Planning Unit in Figures 4-1 through 4-3. The precise locations of the Stage I sample units are provided in Appendix II (unpublished).

C. Sampling Design Rationale: Stage I

The sampling design outlined above involved stratification by three environmental variables: landform, vegetation and water resources. These particular variables were selected because I considered them to have been important factors in prehistoric and/or historic human activity and because they covary with other factors (e.g. soil characteristics) which were perhaps equally important.

The specific categories selected for each variable were chosen because they were considered distinctly relevant, and because their measurement was facilitated by data available on the topographic maps. Other variables and/or categories have been excluded from consideration either because they were judged less relevant or were less readily measurable.

The guidelines employed in the distribution of sampling units among the various stratification categories were designed to help guarantee that each poorly-represented category in the sampling universe would receive at least minimal attention in the overall sample. More specifically, these procedures insured that at least three units were inventoried per category, provided the category was represented by at least three sections.

I initially decided to single out particular areas that were poorly-represented in the sampling universe for one of two basic reasons: either the area was one in which I expected, on the basis of existing evidence, that site densities would be especially high (e.g. spring locations and mesquite zones) or the area was one in which site characteristics and densities were highly problematical (e.g. tank areas and the Amargosa River basin), thus posing a valid and potentially useful research and management question in itself.

In evaluating the stratification design and the distribution of sample units within categories, it is important for the reader to recognize that a number of the more important environmental categories (e.g. mesquite, springs, juniper/piñon) are very poorly-represented within the sampling universe in terms of relative area coverage; so much so, in fact, that it is doubtful that a pure random sampling would have successfully placed units within many of these (exact probabilities may be determined from Table 4-1).

Given that it seemed essential to guarantee the systematic inclusion of such areas in the sample, the question became one of deciding how much of the sample should be devoted to them. On the one hand, I recognized that small sub-samples would produce an analytical problem, precluding their direct use in the estimation of meaningful site frequency parameters. On the other hand, I did not feel that larger sub-sample sizes in the under-represented areas would be consistent with the general and exploratory nature of ARID-I. That is, since the principal objective of the project was an _overall_ cultural resource assessment of the _entire_ Northeast Mojave region, and since the archaeology of the area was poorly understood prior to ARID-I, it seemed appropriate that the majority of the Stage I sample should consist of a comparatively wide-based (in terms of area representation) sample.

In the long-run, the latter reasoning won out and as a result the bulk of the total Stage I sample (over two/thirds) was devoted to a pure random sample of the two areal types most widely-represented in the project area (i.e. "valley/other vegetation/other water resources" and "mountain/other vegetation/other water resources"). In addition, I was confident that the two largest sub-samples could provide strong baseline statistics (with respect to site densities, etc.) against which the smaller sub-samples from the less-well-represented categories could be compared, thus indirectly eliminating some of the analytical problems mentioned earlier. Much the same result could be achieved by pooling sample units (across categories) in other portions of the analysis. The use of these two techniques will become clear in Chapter 7, which examines the results of the analysis.

The sample sizes, both overall and within stages, and the size of the sampling units themselves were recommended by the BLM. The orientation of the sampling units in a north-south direction was chosen to facilitate their description and navigation, and because this orientation would tend to provide greater environmental homogeneity within sample units than would an east-west orientation.

D. Stage II Objectives

In the development of the Stage II Sampling Design, it was determined that it would be disadvantageous to again use a stratified random sample of the total project area, as had been done in the case of Stage I. There were several reasons underlying this decision:

1. Preliminary analysis of the Stage I data indicated that site densities in most mountain regions were quite low: only a handful of sites in these areas had been located and nearly all of these were found in canyon areas rather than the mountains themselves.

    Whenever the frequency of observation of some topic phenomenon (in this case, cultural resource sites) within a given sampling category (e.g. the mountains) is unacceptably low for analytical purposes, a researcher might reasonably resort to one of two alternatives: either he/she might boost the sample size for that category (i.e. bias the sample in favor of mountain units), in the hope of generating a sufficiently large number of observations _or_ he/she might decide to eliminate the category from futher sampling, reasoning that sample units are better spent in categories where they produce a higher frequency of observation.

In developing the Stage II Sample, I chose to follow the latter alternative. Time and economic constraints effectively limited the research to a total sample size of 1% (approximately 210 sampling units) and I felt that, with such a small overall sample available, further sampling in mountain regions would eventually detract from our ability to accurately describe the distribution of sites throughout the project area. The Stage II Sample thus concentrated specifically on valley-pediment areas.

2. Random sampling within a complex environment has the tendency to produce a lot of analytical "noise" in the sense that the environmental characteristics of sampling units drawn from distinct regions usually differ along a multitude of dimensions. This fact often makes it difficult to single out those variables which can best account for the observed variability in the topic phenomenon, even with the aid of multivariate techniques and computer analysis. The Stage II sampling technique was designed to eliminate much of this "noise," by artificially holding certain environmental variables more or less constant, while permitting others to vary over a wide range.

3. As is characteristic of most random samples, the Stage I sample left several areas within the total project area noticeably under-represented. And, it is a near certainty that further random sampling would have failed to adequately represent at least some of these areas. The Stage II sample was designed to concentrate largely on these previously under-represented areas.

4. The dispersed nature of the Stage I sample left most questions concerning the dispersion of cultural resource sites unanswered. The Stage II sample, which involves a form of cluster sampling, was designed in part to deal with the issue of site dispersion.

In addition to the above considerations, I wanted to set up a Stage II Sampling Design that would permit the examination of a problem that was relatively specific and manageable in nature, and yet would be of substantial importance in determining the distribution of sites throughout much of the project area. The problem which I eventually selected was to identify the changes in past human activity (as evidenced in cultural resource sites) which occur as one moves from the floor of a given valley to the upper pediment region; that is, to determine the distribution and attributes of sites in relation to the typical valley cross-section (In part, this problem-focus was inspired by preliminary analysis of the Stage I data, which suggests that most sites tend to occupy areas at or near the valley floor or upper pediment). Theoretically, I believed that this pattern might reflect the fact that ecotonal areas are energy-efficient site locations if access to resources in neighboring environmental zones is critical (This argument will be outlined in greater detail in Chapter 7). I felt that if one could make meaningful statements about this possible relationship, these could be applied throughout most of the project area, and could provide considerable insight to the more general question of why sites exhibit particular distribution and density patterns.

E. The Block Sampling Strategy

To deal with this problem of valley site distribution, I employed a technique which may be called "block sampling." A form of cluster sampling, block sampling involves the selection of a series of territorial "blocks" (or areas), and the systematic placement of sample units within each block. The rationale behind block sampling is comparatively simple. By limiting sampling to relatively restricted areas (blocks), one can effectively maintain quasi-experimental control over many environmental variables, in that these remain more or less constant throughout the block (i.e. all possible sampling units within a restricted block of territory share a number of environmental characteristics in common). The controlling effect of block sampling, in turn, permits a more effective evaluation of the influence of environmental factors which do vary within the block. Of course, one would generally set up a block sampling design with the objective of holding exogenous (or secondary) variables constant, while allowing topic variables (i.e. those of principal interest to the researcher) to change.

Block sampling is highly conducive to analysis of variance techniques. While some topic variables may be held constant within blocks, they may be permitted to vary across blocks. Thus, it is possible, using analysis of variance and block sampling, to isolate the effects of variables which change within blocks from those which vary across blocks, and to evaluate their interactive effect on the dependent phenomenon.

It is important to make clear that in block sampling it is not assumed that a given block is representative of the particular area in which it lies. Any generalizations made about a specific area on the basis of block sampling within that area should be made with considerable caution, since the block itself is not selected randomly from the area. But block sampling is not designed to make such generalizations; rather it is designed to make statements about relationships between site types and distributions, on the one hand, and specific environmental variables, on the other.

Of course, one would normally want to be able to employ block sampling data to make general statements about the entire sampling universe. In order to do so, two factors are critical:

1. The researcher should make an effort to insure that the environmental variability within or between blocks approximates the total environmental variability in the sampling universe. Thus, it is invariably important to sample <u>several</u> blocks which are substantially <u>different</u>.

2. There should be available data from a random sample of the total sampling universe against which to test any generalizations drawn from the analysis of the block sampling data. For the present project, the Stage I sample will serve this purpose quite well (In general, I would think that block sampling should not be employed in the absence of a complementary random sample. It might also be noted that there is at least one advantage in using block sampling <u>after</u> [rather than before] random sampling, since this permits the researcher to place blocks in areas which were under-represented in the random sample).

F. Sampling Design Specifics

Given the particular research problem that had been selected for investigation, the specific independent variable which I wanted to see vary within blocks was <u>valley</u> contour. Thus, it was important to select blocks and sample within them in such a fashion that sampling units occupied a variety of different positions in the valley cross-section. Accordingly, the following block characteristics and sampling procedures were developed:

1. Blocks would consist of sets of contiguous cadastral sections. The cadastral system would be employed to maintain conformity with Stage I procedures and with the overall BLM desert study plan.

2. Blocks would run lengthwise from the upper pediment of a given valley (For simplicity, the Stage I rule, that the upper pediment ends where the slope begins to exceed 600 feet per mile, or 6.5°, was employed) to the valley floor. The block would continue to the upper pediment on the opposite side of the valley, provided this lies within the project area.

3. Between 8 and 12 units (each 1/8 x 1 mile), inclusive, would be sampled per block. The lower limit of 8 was established to insure sufficient data per block for analytical purposes; the upper limit (12) was designed to guarantee that a number of blocks could be sampled with the remaining number of sampling units (68; a total of 69 units were eventually selected).

4. Block width and sampling procedures within blocks would be a function of block length and the limits on sample size set in 3. above. Blocks would generally be one section wide and would contain one sample unit per section. Especially short blocks would be <u>two</u> sections wide to insure that the minimum sample size per block was achieved; <u>every</u> <u>other</u> section would

be sampled in exceptionally long blocks, where the maximum
sample size per block would otherwise be exceeded.

5. Sample units would conform to the cadastral system, as in
   Stage I, and would be oriented either north/south or east/
   west so as to be approximately parallel with existing contours of ground elevation. This orientation procedure would
   be employed since it is important to maintain the sampling
   unit as a manageable analytical unit, which is impractical
   if the sampling unit crosses environmental zones. It was
   assumed, of course, that environmental zones covary with
   elevation contours.

6. A systematic sampling procedure would be employed to insure
   the maximum dispersion of sampling units within blocks.
   First, a single section would be randomly selected within
   each block. Then, a zone within that section would be
   selected, again randomly (As in Stage I, there are 8 zones
   per section, each 1/8 x 1 mile, and numbered 1 to 8, moving
   either from west to east or from north to south, depending
   upon the orientation chosen for sampling units within the
   block). In blocks that are one section wide, each sampled
   section would contain a sampling unit in the same zone; for
   blocks that are two sections wide, the placement of units
   within each row of sections will be staggered (i.e. offset
   by +4 zones), again to insure the maximum dispersion of
   sample units. The pattern of sample unit placement for
   each type of block is shown in Figure 4-4.

G. Block Selection

   In the selection of the blocks themselves, three basic
criteria were employed:

1. Areas were selected which were poorly represented in the
   Stage I sample.

2. An effort was made to place blocks in valleys which differed
   substantially with respect to environmental variables which
   were considered important determinants of site variability.
   For example, some blocks border playas, the Amargosa River,
   or mesquite zones, while others contain springs or are adjacent to mountain ranges with juniper/piñon stands.

3. Blocks were selected with the idea of attempting to limit
   their internal environmental variability as much as possible,
   with the exception of variability directly related to changes
   in valley contour.

   Using the above criteria, seven blocks were selected for implementation of the Stage II Sampling Design. The dimensions and
characteristics of these blocks are described in Table 4-3.
Approximate sample unit locations are provided in Figures 4-1

through 4-3. Precise locations of the Stage II units are listed in Appendix III (unpublished).

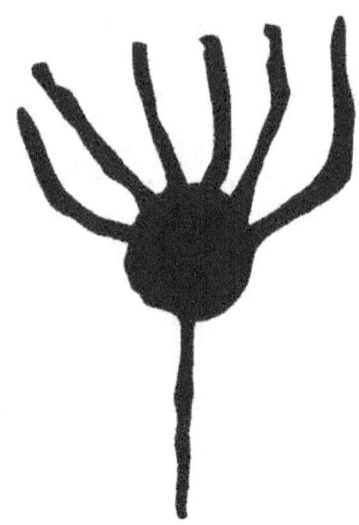

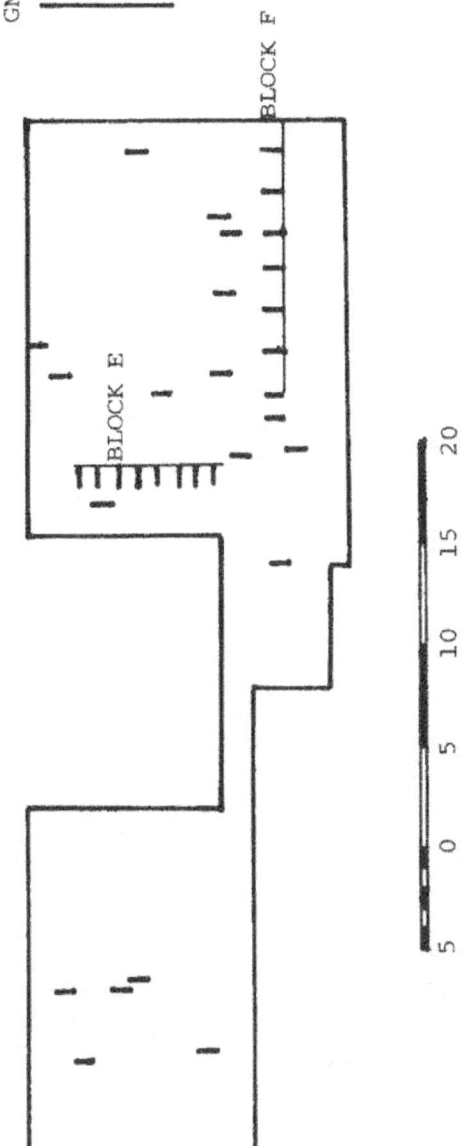

FIGURE 4-1

Owlshead/Amargosa Planning Unit (Northern Half):
Sample Unit Locations

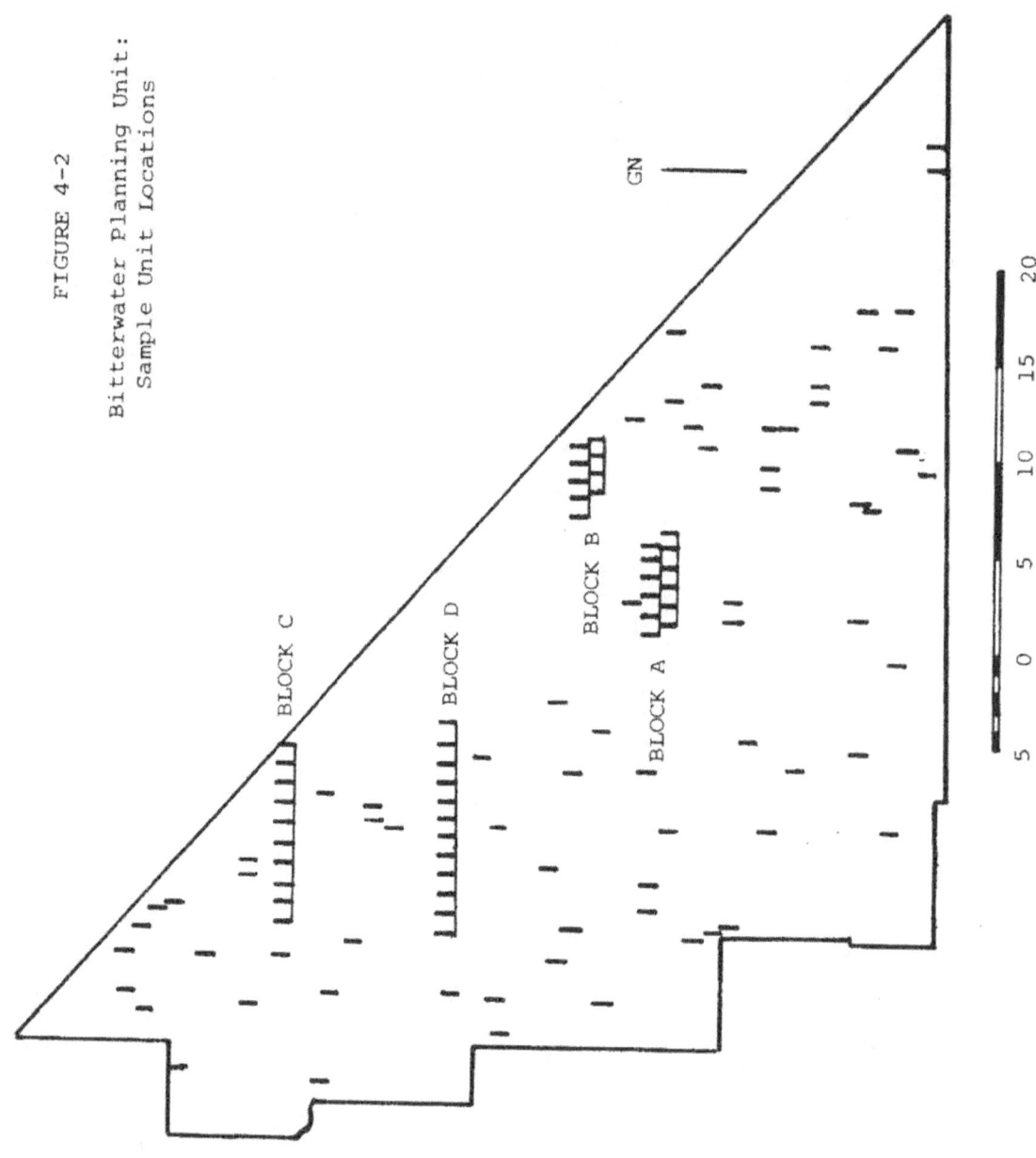

FIGURE 4-2

Bitterwater Planning Unit:
Sample Unit Locations

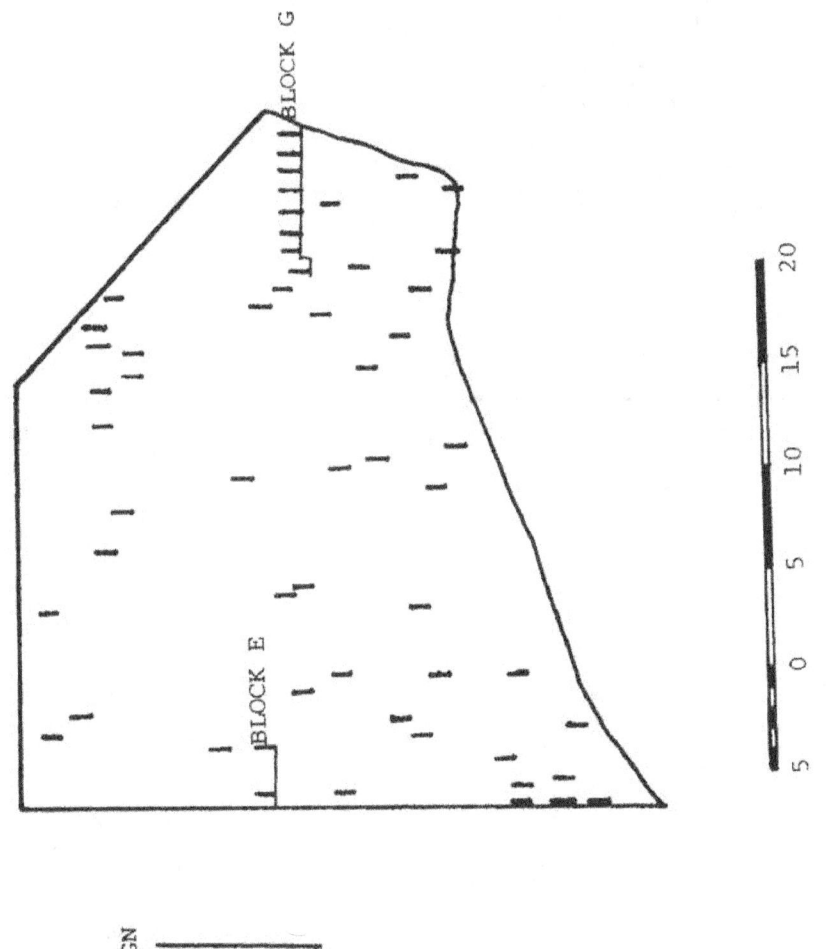

FIGURE 4-3

Kingston Planning Unit: Sample Unit Locations

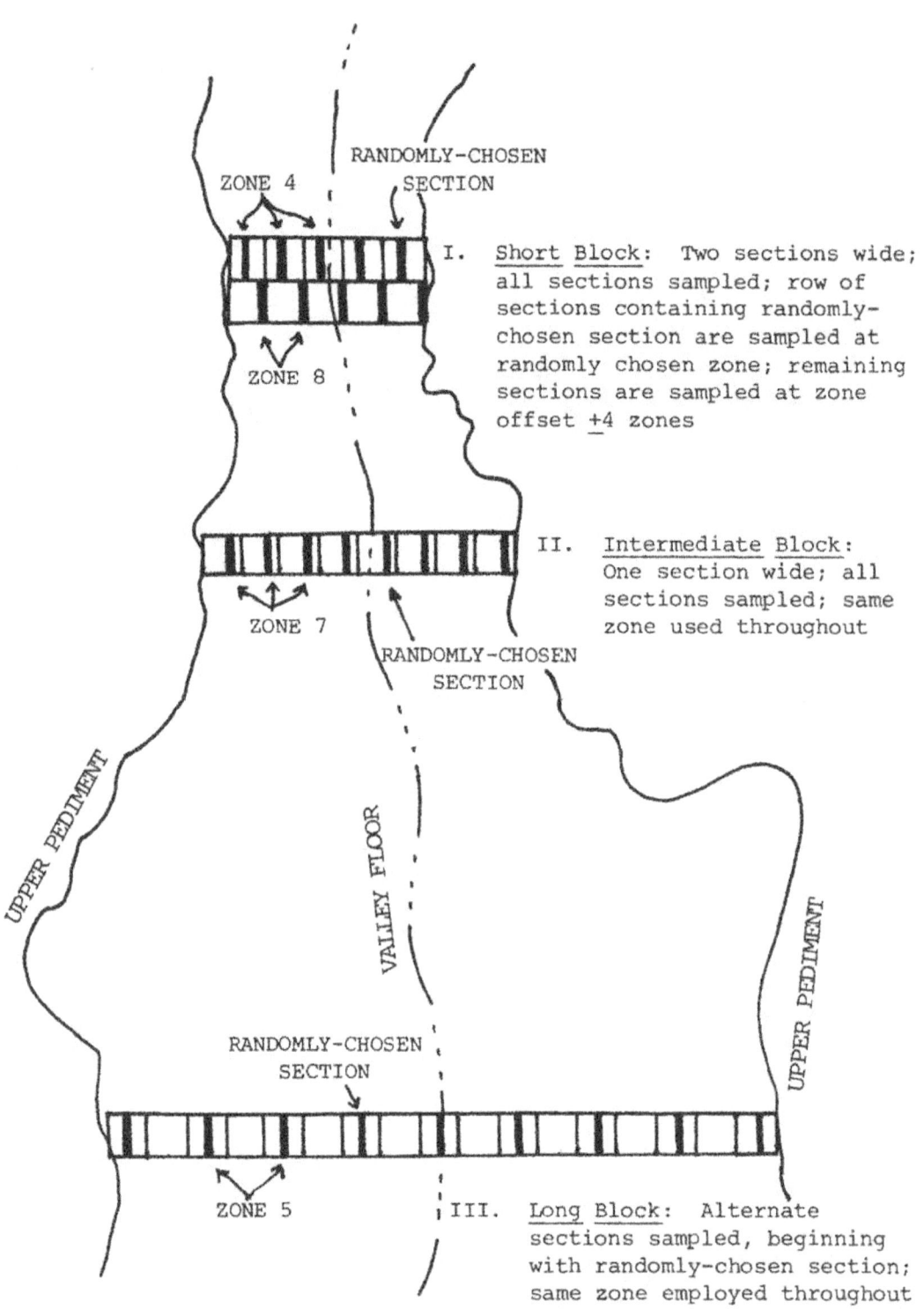

I. Short Block: Two sections wide; all sections sampled; row of sections containing randomly-chosen section are sampled at randomly chosen zone; remaining sections are sampled at zone offset ±4 zones

II. Intermediate Block: One section wide; all sections sampled; same zone used throughout

III. Long Block: Alternate sections sampled, beginning with randomly-chosen section; same zone employed throughout

FIGURE 4-4

Block Configurations and Sample Unit Placement

-42-

TABLE 4-1

Assignment of Sections to Stratification Categories

VEGETATION	WATER RESOURCES	Mountain	Valley	Playa	Total
Juniper/piñon	Amargosa River	1			1
	Wells and reservoirs	39			39
	Other water resources				
	Total	40			40
Mesquite	Amargosa River				
	Wells and reservoirs		6		6
	Tanks				
	Springs		23	13	36
	Other water resources				
	Total		29	13	42
Other Vegetation	Amargosa River	10	81	5	96
	Wells and reservoirs	2	28	1	31
	Tanks	1	3		4
	Springs	23	20		43
	Other Water resources	773	1648	37	2458
	Total	809	1780	43	2532
	Grand Total	849	1809	56	2714

LANDFORM

TABLE 4-2

STAGE I SAMPLING UNITS BY STRATIFICATION CATEGORY

LANDFORM

VEGETATION	WATER RESOURCES	Mountain	Valley	Playa	Total
Juniper/piñon	Amargosa River	1 (12.5)			1 (12.5)
	Wells and reservoirs				
	Tanks				
	Springs				
	Other water resources	4 (1.28)			4 (1.28)
	Total	5 (1.56)			5 (1.56)
Mesquite	Amargosa River		3 (6.25)		3 (6.25)
	Wells and reservoirs				
	Tanks				
	Springs				
	Other water resources		3 (1.63)	3 (2.88)	6 (2.08)
	Total		6 (2.59)	3 (2.88)	9 (2.67)
Other Vegetation	Amargosa River	3 (3.75)	7 (1.08)	3 (7.5)	13 (1.69)
	Wells and reservoirs	2 (12.5)	3 (1.34)	1 (12.5)	6 (2.42)
	Tanks	1 (12.5)	3 (12.5)		4 (12.5)
	Springs	3 (1.63)	3 (1.88)		9 (2.62)
	Other water resources	26 (0.42)	68 (0.52)	3 (1.01)	94 (0.48)
	Total	35 (0.54)	84 (0.59)	7 (2.03)	126 (0.60)
	Grand Total	40 (0.59)	90 (0.62)	10 (2.23)	140 (0.64)

(Values in parentheses indicate sample size as a percent of the total number of sections, or approximate area, assigned to each stratification category.)

-44-

TABLE 4-3

STAGE II SAMPLING DESIGN INFORMATION

BLOCK DESIGNATION	GENERAL LOCATION	MAP	BLOCK WIDTH	SECTIONS SAMPLED	TRANSECT ORIENTATION	SAMPLE SIZE
A	Chicago Valley	Stewart Valley	2	all	n/s	12
B	Pahrump Valley	Stewart Valley	2	all	n/s	9
C	Upper Amargosa	Ash Meadows	1	all	n/s	11
D	Middle Amargosa	Eagle Mountain	1	all	n/s	12
E	Lower Amargosa	Shoshone/ Avawatz Pass	1	all	e/w	8
F	Kingston Wash/ Valjean Valley	Silurian Hills/ Kingston Peak	1	alternate	n/s	9
G	Ivanpah	Clark Mountain/ Roach Lake	1	all	n/s	8

CHAPTER 5. FIELD IMPLEMENTATION

A. The Field Experience

The ARID-I fieldwork was conducted, for the most part, from
a series of outdoor base camps. These base camps would be maintained for periods up to one week in duration, depending upon the
number of sample units within the vicinity; the camp would be moved
whenever the sample units in that area had been exhausted. Each
new base camp would be chosen so as to minimize the distances to
a maximum number of un-inventoried sample units, as well as to
provide comfortable camping conditions. Like many hunter-gatherer
and pastoralist peoples (see, for example, Lee 1969; Barth 1961),
ours was a truly nomadic existence, with movements governed by
the availability of our "critical resources" (that is, sample
units).

Living conditions in the field were meager at best. Crew
members cooked on Coleman stoves and slept in the open or in the
back of the survey vehicles; a tent had been employed early in
the course of the fieldwork, but was soon abandoned due to unpredictable wind conditions and several predictably bad experiences
resulting from these conditions. Since no refrigeration facilities
(other than Mother Nature) were available, most meals came straight
from the can.

The possibility of vandalism was a constant problem; thus
very little equipment was ever left at the base camp when the
crews departed for the day's work. Much time was thus spent
loading materials (cooking equipment, sleeping gear, etc.) into
the survey vehicles in the morning and unloading them when the
crews returned at night.

Most daylight hours were generally expended conducting the
inventory itself. The remainder was spent at rest or preparing
equipment, forms, maps, and crews for the following day's work.

On occasion, deviations from the above routine were possible.
While working in the Shoshone area, for example, the field crew
spent several days living in one of the more well-appointed caves
for which the region is famous. Several nights were also spent
with friends living in Death Valley Junction. Whenever we were
near Tecopa or one of the few other small communities which dot
the project area, most of the crew would readily opt for a restau-
rant-cooked meal or an ice-cold drink. Entertainment highlights
included the Mountain Pass Bowling Alley, the Death Valley Junction
Belly-Dancing Class and Joe's Stateline Saloon.

Socially speaking, the members of the crew fared quite well,
although the sudden flare-up of temper, which one must learn to
expect whenever a number of people are thrown together in a hostile
environment, was an occasional occurrence.

The typical week included five working days and four nights in the field, although the unusual precipitation of the spring of 1978 meant several shorter periods and much frustration. When the work week was over, the entire field crew would retire to Las Vegas, where those of us who were non-residents would spend long hours losing our hard-earned money at slot machines and other vices, while the remainder intelligently slept.

Privately-owned vehicles were used exclusively throughout the fieldwork. Fortunately, we were plagued with few break-downs or other vehicle mishaps. "Ichi-ban," Crabtree's tireless (in more ways than one) Datsun pick-up and "Moby Dick," Claude Warren's amazing Dodge Power Wagon, deserve special recognition.

In all, the ARID-I fieldwork spanned a five-month period, from November 2, 1977 through March 29, 1978. Fortunately, this proved to be an excellent time of year for desert work, despite the extensive spring rains. Daytime temperatures were mild, nights were cold but not excessively so, and wind velocities generally had little impact on the progress of the work.

B. Personnel

At the initiation of fieldwork, we experimented with the idea of deploying two 2-person crews during the week and up to six crews on the weekend, when additional personnel could be secured. This proved undesirable from an organizational standpoint and the idea was soon abandoned. For the remainder of the fieldwork, a maximum of three 2-member crews were utilized.

The individuals participating in the fieldwork included: R. Crabtree, G. Coombs, R. McCarty, T. Shepperson, S. Crownover, C. Warren Jr., E. Crabtree, M. Plyler, D. Tublitz, K. August, K. Greene, L. Abernathy, P. Baratti and M. Hensen. Eric Ritter of the BLM Desert Planning Staff joined the field crew for brief periods during both stages of the inventory providing valuable input and contributing to the field effort.

Most of the above took part only during the early "experimental weekends." The bulk of the fieldwork was conducted by R. Crabtree, Coombs, Crownover, Tublitz, Abernathy and Warren.

C. Standard Inventory Procedures

As described in Chapter 4, sample units were 1 mile long, 1/8 mile wide and oriented either north-south or east-west. In general, the following methods were employed to inventory each such unit.

1. The sample unit would be traversed lengthwise, on foot, by a two-person crew. The crew would consist of the crew chief and assistant. The crew chief would carry a compass and map and would be responsible for the overall orientation of the crew

12. Crews would collect field specimens of lithic materials (unmodified) or plant species which they could not identify. These would be classified upon returning to base camp, either by members of other crews or with the aid of a variety of field manuals.

D. Deviations from Typical Inventory Methods

Occasionally it would be necessary to depart from the above-outlined procedures. The following represent some of the more important alterations.

1. One day in the field, the wind was blowing so strongly from the south that it proved impossible to complete a survey sweep in a southerly direction. In this case, a four-member crew, using the standard fifty meter spacing, completed a single northerly sweep across that day's sample units. This same method was also used on other occasions where terrain features, road locations or other considerations made a single four-person sweep the more feasible or efficient alternative.

2. Frequently, the sweep pattern was inititated at some point other than at one end of the sample unit. In these cases, the survey pattern would invariably run from the starting point to one end of the unit, then to the far end, and finally to the starting point once again. This variant form is amply documented in the ARID-I Sample Unit Records.

3. Frequently, portions of the site and sample unit records would not be completed until the crew returned to the base camp. This was particularly likely when time or other constraints limited the period that the crew could remain in the field or when the classification of cultural or natural items required consultation with other crew members.

4. In a few instances, it proved impossible to inventory all of the surface area of a particular sample unit. Steep terrain and the presence of water or other physical obstacles were generally the determining factors involved. In these cases, territory adjoining the original sample unit were substituted by the crew involved; these adjacent lands were surveyed as if they were the sample units themselves.

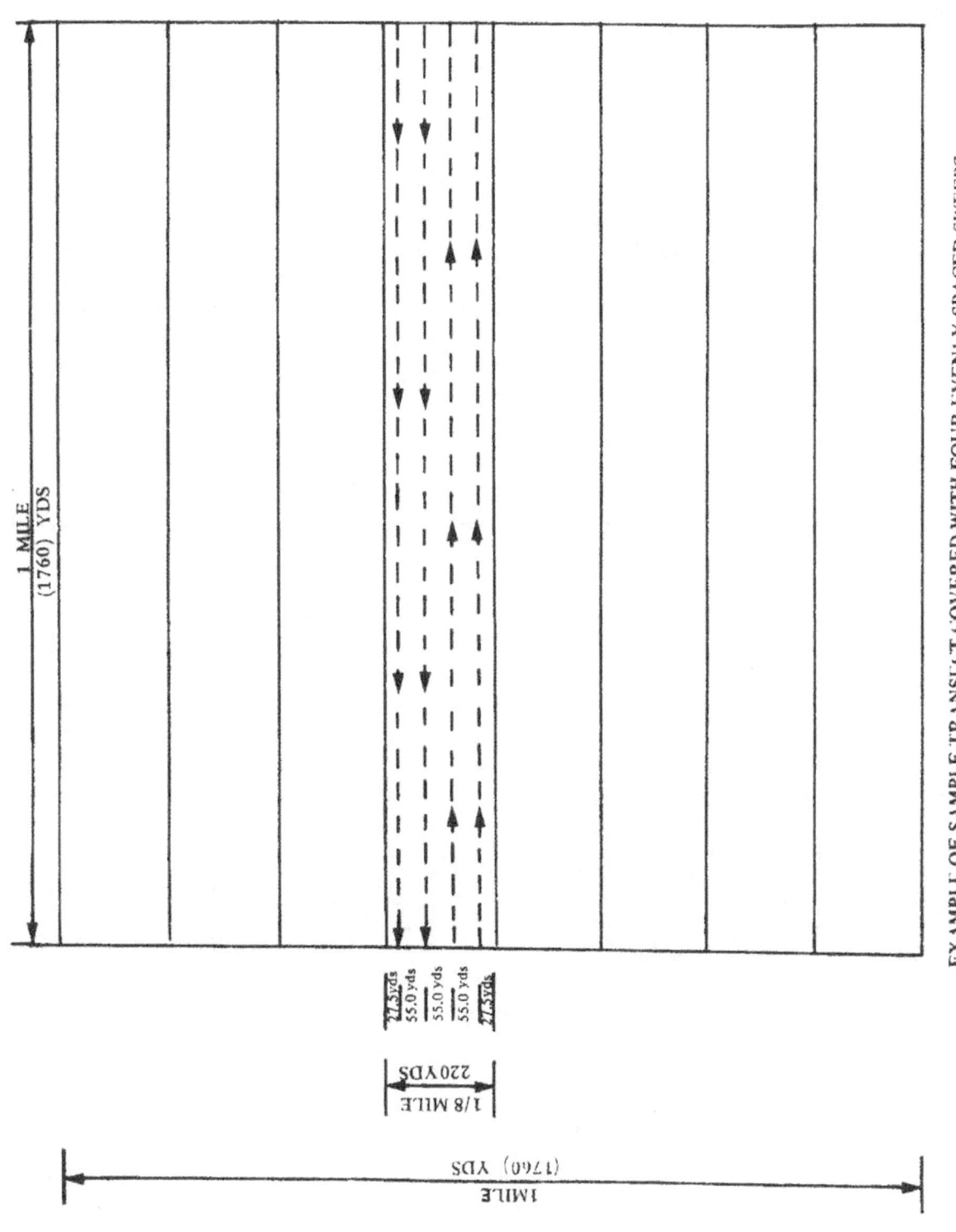

FIGURE 5-1.   SURVEY PATH (IDEALIZED)

FIGURE 5-2

ARCHAEOLOGICAL PHOTOGRAPHIC RECORD

YEAR		FILM TYPE		CAMERA & LENS TYPE	FILM SPEED	DAY	TUNG	PAGE NO.	

Mo.	Day	Time	Exp. Frame	SUBJECT	SITE NO.	Cat. No.
			1		05 -	
			2		05 -	
			3		05 -	
			4		05 -	
			5		05 -	
			6		05 -	
			7		05 -	
			8		05 -	
			9		05 -	
			10		05 -	
			11		05 -	
			12		05 -	
			13		05 -	
			14		05 -	
			15		05 -	
			16		05 -	
			17		05 -	
			18		05 -	
			19		05 -	
			20		05 -	
			21		05 -	
			22		05 -	
			23		05 -	
			24		05 -	

BLM CALIFORNIA DESERT PROJECT
ARCHAEOLOGICAL SITE SURVEY RECORD

[1] County	_____
[2] District	_____
[3] Planning Unit	_____
[4] Sample Unit	_____
[5] Photos	_____
[6] Date	_____
[7] Recorder	_____

[8] Site # _____ [9] Other # _____

[10] Site Name _____

[11] Cadastral Location: Twn _____ Rng _____ _____ of _____ of Sec _____

[12] Quadrangle _____ [13] Elevation _____

[14] UTM Grid Loc. Zone _____ Northing _____ Easting _____

[15] Reference Points: _____
_____

[16] OWNER	[17] NAT'L REGISTER	[18] DISTURB	[19] CNDT	[20] COMMENTS

[16] OWNER: BLM, OTHER FED., STATE, PRIVATE, UNKNOWN

[17] NAT'L REGISTER:
(A) STATUS: LISTED, CANDIDATE, POTENTIAL, NOT ELG., NO DET.
(B) TYPE: DISTRICT, SITE, OTHER

[18] DISTURB: DEVELOPMENT, ANIMAL, VANDALISM, ORV, OTHER

[19] CNDT: GOOD, FAIR, POOR

[20] COMMENTS:

[21] SITE TYPES: VILLAGE, TEMPORARY CAMP, SHELTER/CAVE, MILLING STA., LITHIC SCATTER, QUARRY SITE, POTTERY LOCUS, CEMETERY, CREMATION LOCUS, INTAGLIO, ROCK ALIGNMENT, PETROGLYPH, PICTOGRAPH, TRAIL, ROASTING PIT, ISOLATED FIND, CAIRN, HISTORIC, OTHER

[22] AREA: 0-10 Sq. M., 11-50, 51-250, 251-1000, 1001-5000, over 5000

[23] DEPTH: SURFACE, 1-20 Cm., 21-100, over 100, UNKNOWN

[24] General Site Description:

[25] FEATURES: STRUCTURAL DEP., ROCK RING, ROCK STRUCTURE, CAIRN/SHRINE, ROASTING PIT/FAR, HEARTH, PETROGLYPHS, PICTOGRAPHS, BEDROCK MORTAR, GRINDING SLICK, OTHER

[26] ARTIFACTS: PROJECTILE POINT, FLAKED STONE TOOL, CORE-DETRITUS, MILLING TOOL, OTHER GROUND STONE, CERAMIC, BONE, PERISHABLE, ORNAMENT, HISTORIC, OTHER

[27] ECO.: FIRE AFFECTED ROCK, FAUNA, FLORA, OTHER

[28] MAT.: CRYPTOCRYSTALLINE, OBSIDIAN, FELSITE, OTHER

[29] Describe:

FIGURE 5-3 A

-53-

[30] VEGETATION

BARREN	SALTBUSH	CREOSOTE	JOSHUA/CREOSOTE	JOSHUA/YUCCA	YUCCA/CACTUS	BLACKBRUSH	SAGEBRUSH	PINYON/JUNIPER	CONIFER	SHADSCALE	CHAPARRAL	OAK WOODLAND	MESQUITE	RIPARIAN	WASH	GRASSLAND	OTHER

[31] COVERAGE

CONTINUOUS (over75%)	INTERRUPTED (50-75%)	PARK-LIKE (25-50%)	RARE (6-25%)	BARELY PRESENT (1-5%)	ABSENT (0-1%)

[32] WATER

INTERMITTENT STREAM	PERMANENT STREAM	SPRING	PLAYA	OTHER

[33] Describe

[34] LANDFORM

MOUNTAIN	HILL	TERRACE	RIDGE	ALLUVIAL FAN	CANYON	ARROYO	SAND DUNE	DESERT PAVEMENT	BADLANDS	PLAYA	OTHER

[35] BEDROCK

EXTRUSIVE IG.	INTRUSIVE IG.	METAMORPHIC	SEDIMENTARY	QUATERNARY ALLUV.	OTHER

[36] TEXTURE

SAND	LOAM	SILT	CLAY	OTHER

[37] SOILS

MIDDEN	ALLUVIAL	COLLUVIAL	EOLIAN	BEDROCK	OTHER

[38] Describe

[39] SLOPE

POINT OF INFLEX	LOWER 1/3	MID 1/3	UPPER 1/3	0-5°	6-15°	16-30°	31-60°	over 60°

[40] ASPECT

NORTH	NORTH/EAST	EAST	SOUTH/EAST	SOUTH	SOUTH/WEST	WEST	NORTH/WEST

[41] EROSION

DEFLATION	RILLING	GULLYING	SHEET/WASH	ROCK/DEBRIS	SLUMPING	OTHER

[42] DRAIN.

CONVERGING	DIVERGING	BRAIDED	OTHER

[43] Remarks

BLM CALIFORNIA DESERT PROJECT
HISTORIC SITE SURVEY FORM

```
County     _____
District   _____
Planning Unit _____
Sample Unit _____
Photos     _____
Date       _____
Recorder   _____
```

1. Site Number _____ 2. Site Name _____

3. Other (numbers/names) _____

4. Location: Twn ____, Rng ____, ____of
   ____, of Sec ____, Quad _____, Elev _____

   Reference Points: _____

   _____

   UTM Grid Loc: Zone _____ North _____ East _____

5. Ownership: BLM __, Other Federal __, State __, Private __, Unk __,

6. National Register Status: Candidate __, Potential __, Determined
                             not Elgible __, No Determination __,

7. Disturbance: Animal __, Burning __, Vandalism __, ORV __,
                Other __, Explain_____

   _____

8. Present Condition: Good __, Fair __, Poor __, Explain _____

   _____

9. Activity: Mining __, Railroad __, Military __, Homesteading __,
             Exploration/Traveling __, Settlement __, Ranching __,
             Other __, Explain _____

10. Site Type: Town __, Camp __, Homestead __, Road __, Trail __,
               Mine __, Railroad __, Graveyard __, Trashdump __,
               Military __, Other _____

11. Features: Structure __, Dugout __, Fire Hearth __, Cairn __,
              Rock Alignment __, Trashdump __, Irrigation __,
              Trail __, Road __, Corral __, Burial __, Well __,
              Spring __, R&R Grade (berm) __, Tram (road/way) __,
              Tailings __, Other __, Explain _____

   _____

12. Artifacts: Wood (size,type) __, Glass (color) __, Metal (type) __,
               Bone (species) __, Ceramic (color) __, Adobe (con-
               dition) __, Nails (size,type) __, Cans (size,type) __,
               Ordnance __, Other___, Explain _____

   _____

13. Temporal Period: Circa _____, Era _____

(continue on reverse side,
refer by number)

FIGURE 5-4

CALIFORNIA DESERT PROGRAM
ARCHAEOLOGICAL SAMPLE UNIT RECORD

1. Planning Unit_____ 2. Sample Unit #_____ 3. Date_____

4. Twp._____ Range_____ Section_____ 5. Map_____

6. General Location:

7. Vegetation:

8. Fauna:

9. Geology/Geomorphology:

10. Hydrology:

11. Weather Conditions:

12. Sites Recorded:

13. Duration of Survey:

14. Survey Crew:

Recorder:_____

FIGURE 5-5 A

15. <u>General Interpretations & Comments</u> (Attach additional pages as necessary):

16. <u>Sketch Map of Sample Unit</u> Indicate: a) Dimensions of sample unit;
b) Pertinent or prominant land forms; c) Survey pattern, including
approximate area covered and portion of unit covered by individual
crew members; d) Location of sites recorded.

FIGURE 5-5 B

CHAPTER 6. VALIDITY AND RELIABILITY

The terms validity and reliability frequently appear in archaeological reports, but seldom accompanied by the conceptual rigor
that characterizes their application in disciplines, like psychology, where measurement has become a dominant concern. The concepts of validity and reliability can be of considerable value
to archaeological research, however, and warrant a more detailed
treatment for, as we shall see, they can provide a number of
critical contributions to the evaluation and interpretation of
all aspects of a management and research program.

This chapter is concerned with the validity and reliability
of the research procedures developed and utilized in ARID-I. The
main objectives of the chapter will be to define and discuss these
concepts and to identify their importance to the present work.
Hopefully, in the process, their utility to archaeological research and cultural resource management in general will also become evident. Let us begin with an examination of the validity
concept.

A. Validity

In general terms, the concept of validity is concerned with
what a particular research tool accomplishes. Practically any
research instrument may be examined with respect to its validity;
thus we may question the validity of an operational definition,
of a typology or other measurement/classification scheme, the
validity of a statistical test or of our formal logic, the validity of an entire research design, and so on. In each case,
validity refers to the degree to which the tool under examination
does what we want it to. Thus, for example, we may ask whether
it is valid to use Pearson correlation as a means of determining
the strength of association between two variables measured along
an ordinal scale. The answer would be no, since this particular
statistical test is designed exclusively for interval-scale data
and will not accurately describe associations between other types
of variables; the test is invalid because it does not accomplish
what we want.

In examining the overall validity of a research plan, it is
often useful to begin with an investigation of topic phenomena
and their respective operational definitions. In ARID-I, the
main dependent variable is the cultural resource site. Many
archaeologists would nominally define such a site as a spatial
locus where past human behavior took place. This nominal definition may be made somewhat more precise by demanding that "past
behavior" means "behavior occurring over 50 (or 75, or 100) years
ago" or "before 1930"; in fact without this built-in time lag the
scrupulous archaeological survey crew would be forced to record
its own inventory path as a site upon the completion of each

sample unit.(Although this may seem overly zealous to some, we shall see that conscientiousness in the formulation of nominal definitions is oftentimes critical to the development of a valid piece of research.)

An _operational_ definition refers to the physical or other _evidence_ that will be used to identify the topic phenomenon _as it has been nominally defined_ (This is a somewhat narrower connotation for the term "operational definition" than is normally employed, but is convenient for illustrative purposes; see Kerlinger, 1964: 34-38, for a more commonly-used definition). In ARID-I, the cultural resource site has been operationally defined as a spatial locus exhibiting, on its surface, either:

1. Items judged to have been physically modified by human behavior (Such items are normally called "artifacts," "ecofacts," and "detritus" and in the Northeast Mojave region consist primarily of chipping debris, ground stone implements, projectile points, blades, knives, scrapers and other chipped-stone tools, and pottery, together with tin cans, glass and a variety of other more-recent materials) or;

2. Sets of physical items judged to have been structurally _arranged_ as a consequence of human activity. Such sets shall be called "features" (This is a slightly unusual usage but one which I am most comfortable with; note for example that, using this definition, pictographs [or arrows and tin cans] are features, since they are composites, while petroglyphs are artifacts, since they are modified units) and are represented in the ARID-I project area primarily in the form of hearths, cairns, living surfaces, intaglio, wells and buildings.

In general, the BLM Site Classification System (Appendix I) was employed to operationally define specific site types.

In comparing the nominal and operational definitions of a site outlined above, we can immediately identify several actual or potential problems. Let us examine several of the more important of these.

1. It should be observed that the _operational_ definition of a site is concerned only with a series of physical "indicants" whereas the nominal definition presently includes all conceivable types of human behavior, including behaviors such as traveling from one location to another which may not leave such indicants (no prehistoric trails were recorded during the fieldwork). In this sense, the operational definition is invalid with respect to the nominal definition, and one of the two definitions must therefore be revised. Since the archaeologist must ultimately rely on physical indicators of one sort or another, it would obviously be most reasonable to alter the nominal definition to conform with the operational definition. For convenience, we shall postpone these and other

alterations until all validity problems have been identified. It should be noted, however, that our validity check has already begun to qualify the range of cultural phenomena that this research may address itself to.

2. It is possible that certain items may exist within the project area which do not fall within the limited range of acceptable items specified in the operational definition, even though these were in fact modified or arranged as a result of past human behavior. For example, Native American consultants to the BLM Desert Planning Staff have identified a number of artifact and site types (e.g. "prayer stones") which would not be recognized by most archaeologists (Eric Ritter, personal communication). Thus, it is important to recognize that the operational definition makes certain critical limiting assumptions about the nature and formal attributes of cultural remains (in general, these assumptions are implicit and are based on existing archaeological knowledge and the ability of archaeologists to apply that knowledge) and that such assumptions may be invalid.

3. The operational definition suggests that behavior took place where the indicative items are found. There are two validity problems here:

    a. The materials may have been moved as a result of action by the environment - by erosion, flooding, wind activity, etc.. This is a definite case in which some validity is lost, since the loci of present observation and of the original activity do not coincide. This problem is discussed in somewhat greater detail in a note at the end of this chapter.

    b. The items may have been modified or manufactured in one place and then moved by humans to another. In such cases, the locus of observation accurately reflects human activity, but the possibility of such occurrences implies that conclusions drawn concerning site type may be invalid. That is, assuming no other validity problems, an isolated projectile point may serve as a valid indicator of a site, but whether it is a hunting, manufacturing or other type of site may not be as obvious as it seems.

4. Measurement procedures themselves may also have a direct effect on the validity of an operational definition vis-a-vis the nominal definition. The field methods employed in ARID-I followed standard archaeological survey guidelines. Sample units were traversed on foot by observers trained in the identification of archaeological resources; sites were recorded when diagnostic indicants were observed. Again a validity problem immediately presents itself: these procedures must invariably fail to record sites (as they have been nominally defined) if all of the remaining physical evidence is buried beneath the surface of the ground. Thus, the measurement procedures

employed in ARID-I have systematicallly excluded buried sites, and these procedures remain valid only if the nominal definition is modified so that "site" refers exclusively to "surface sites" (I am including "exposed profile indications" in the "surface site" category).

At this point, it may be useful to briefly review what has been accomplished thus far. Our validity check has consisted of a careful (although incomplete) examination of the topic phenomenon, as it has been nominally defined, and the posing of two critical questions:

1. Can we measure this phenomenon and have we done so? We have learned that the answer to this question is no; thoroughly valid measures of the topic phenomenon would have required excavation (in order to locate buried sites) and other techniques too costly, time-consuming or simply unavailable to the archaeologist.

2. Can we make rigorous and meaningful statements about this phenomenon? Again, the answer is no, since we have not obtained valid measures of the phenomenon. Such statements can only be made about phenomenon that are nominally defined in a manner that is consistent with the corresponding operational definitions and measurement procedures.

In short, no meaningful statements relevant to ARID-I can be made about the set of "all past human behavior." The validity review has identified, however, that universe which may be systematically studied. Specifically, statements can be made about past human behavior which:

    a. left physical indicants that are:
    b. recognizable to trained observers, and;
    c. present on the surface of the ground.

The validity analysis has also warned us that we must be cautious of 1) the functions (i.e. the types of behavior) that we ascribe to particular collections of materials classified as sites and of 2) the conclusions we might come to concerning the relationship between the original locus of human activity and the present locus of cultural remains.

Some readers may feel that this discussion has "spoiled" ARID-I, by reducing the site to a comparatively meaningless subset of its original self. To a certain extent, of course, this is correct, but it is equally correct for archaeology in general. As much as we would all like to believe that we are studying "all past behavior," this is simply not the case. Validity analysis merely forces us to admit this fact in recognizing the limitations of our data and our methods, and in doing so it performs an invaluable service.

The validity tests that have been performed thus far in relation to "sites" can also be employed to examine the principal "independent phenomena" of this research - notably environmental variables.

The measurement procedures that were used to identify and differentiate environmental factors were fairly straightforward ones. These involved field observations conducted during the inventory (see Chapter 5), coupled with the use of recent map data on topography, water resources and major vegetation categories (see, for example, Chapter 4). These procedures were used to determine the present natural and physical environments for each inventory unit.

The basic critical assumption in the classification of environments was of course, that there is a general spatial correspondence between present and past environments. The problems associated with this assumption are many and varied. We know that during the Pleistocene and at least once in recent times, the climate of the Northeast Mojave was significantly milder than today, with permanent lakes filling most of its playas, higher biomass and more active rivers, springs and other water systems. From our fieldwork, it is evident not only that seasonal differences in the desert are substantial but also that, within seasons, even year-to-year fluctuations in precipitation and overall climate can be considerable. Collectively, the evidence suggests that the use of present environmental conditions as a means of predicting either past environments or past human activity should be performed with considerable caution.

The presence of datable artifacts and other materials within sites can go a long way toward alleviating such problems, of course, since the corresponding environment may also be reconstructed, at least on a macroscopic level, from geologic and other evidence. Unfortunately, the vast majority of sites in the Northeast Mojave are not easily dated. Accordingly, I follow Bettinger (1977a: 218) in assuming that:

1. The general settlement-subsistence pattern for the research area remained comparatively constant over the period of human occupation, despite known environmental changes, and that;

2. The observed site variability reflects different aspects of this single settlement-subsistence pattern, rather that different patterns occurring sequentially and resulting from environmental changes or other intervening factors (also see Davis, 1963: 204).

Ultimately, of course, dated sites and environmental reconstructions could be employed as a means of testing these assumptions. While such an effort is certainly beyond the scope of ARID-I and impractical given the available resources, the validity of these assumptions can be indirectly estimated, simply by examining the effectiveness of using present environmental variables to predict regional site parameters (see Chapter 7).

The question of validity should also be posed with respect to analytical techniques and the assumptions that underlie them. Ideally speaking, one of the simplest pieces of analysis required in ARID-I involves estimating overall site frequencies. These estimates may be derived directly from the sample means and are valid, provided that 1) the samples are random ones and 2) the measures of site frequencies per sample unit are accurate ones.

As it turns out, assumption 2) proves to be invalid; we now know that the site frequency counts per sample unit tend to consistently underestimate the actual numbers of sites present within these inventory units. Let us see how this is so.

The reader will recall from Chapter 5 that crew members were required, under the contract, to maintain spacing of fifty meters while traversing each sample unit. This would assure a minimization of maximum spacing, assuming that two crew members must cover a 1/8-mile-wide zone in a single up and back sweep.

The adequacy of fifty meter spacing has been justified, at least in part, by Robert Bettinger's survey report of the Long Valley Caldera, Mono County, California. In his report, Bettinger notes that:

> At the outset of the field work, there was
> some question whether 50 m. intervals were suffi-
> ciently small to insure that nearly all sites within
> a tract (i.e. sample unit) would be located. To test
> this possibility, the first five tracts were surveyed
> at 25 m. intervals in one half and 50 m. intervals in
> the other half. Surprisingly, the 50 m. intervals
> located more sites in all five tracts. Although it
> would be foolish - if only on logical grounds - to
> conclude that 50 m. intervals will locate more sites
> than 25 m. intervals, these results tend to support
> the notion that there is no marked difference in the
> rate of site recovery between 25 m. intervals and 50
> m. intervals. (1977b: 16)

Several comments should be made about Bettinger's experiment and the conclusions he derives. First, it should be noted that the sample he employs is quite small, certainly too small to be statistically significant, and thus any conclusions should not be accepted without scepticism.

Secondly, Bettinger does not state whether his experiment was "blind," that is whether his crews were unaware of the objectives of the experiment, or whether sample unit halves were assigned to the "25 m." and "50 m." categories on a random basis. Numer-ous studies in psychology have demonstrated how easily an investi-gator's expectations and desired-results can influence the outcome of an experiment when such controls are not a built-in feature of the experimental design (see, for example, Rosenthal, 1966). Since Bettinger does not discuss these measures, one must assume that they were not employed, particularly since, as he notes, his results are consistently opposite to what one would expect on logical-probabilistic grounds.

Thirdly, if Bettinger used the same number of sweeps and crew members for each half of his experiment, it can be maintained that his results will be true more often than not, but that these results do not support his conclusions. Consider the following argument.

For any idealized site type, there exists some maximum distance at which that type of site can usually be recognized by a trained observer. We may refer to twice this distance as the "observing-range" for that site type. Let us assume, for illustrative purposes, that an isolated metate, 0.3 meters in diameter and lying exposed on the surface of the ground, can be identified at a distance of 20 meters. Thus a trained observer, operating under normal conditions, could see a metate up to a distance of 20 meters to either side of his/her line of march (observing-range = 40 meters).

If two observers are spaced at a distance smaller than the observing range for some site type, then a portion of each observer's observing-range for the two-member crew, as a unit, will be smaller than if the individual observing-ranges did not overlap. In our example, if two crew members were spaced 30 meters apart, then ten meters of their observing-ranges (for metates) would overlap - thus the crew's total observing-range would be only 70 meters. If, on the other hand, they were spaced 40 meters apart, their observing-ranges would touch but not overlap and the total observing-range for the crew would be a full 80 meters (or double the range for each observer). Finally, if crew members are spaced more than 40 meters apart, the total observing-range for the crew would still be 80 meters, but there will be an intervening "blindspot" where neither observer is able to recognize metates.

The reader should understand that the number of sites observed by a crew will be a direct function of its total observing-range (among many other factors, of course). On the one hand, if spacing is less than the observing-range for some site type, efficiency is lower and fewer sites will be recorded (over the long run) than if spacing were equal to the observing-range for one observer. On the other hand, if spacing is equal to or greater than the individual's observing-range, the number of sites recorded would be approximately the same, since the total range for the crew remains constant.

The discussion thus far indicates that Bettinger's experimental results may be logically true but trivial. That is, as crew spacing increases, the number of sites recorded should either increase or remain the same (on the average), depending on whether the original spacing is less than or greater than the observing-range for one observer. Once again, all of this assumes that Bettinger employed the same number of sweeps and crew members for each half of his experiment. Even if he did not, however, the other arguments outlined before still obtain.

In general, if crew members are spaced X meters apart, but the observing-range for one or more site types is less than X, then crews will miss at least a portion of the sites within the area which they are supposed to inventory in full, since their observing-range does not cover the entire surface of the survey unit (The formula, 1-R/S, gives the average proportion of sites of a type visible at a distance R, which one may expect to find using crew spacing equal to S). If, for example, the observing-range for metates is only 40 meters, and 50 meter spacing and the inventory plan identified in Chapter 5 are employed, then an average of 20% of all metates within sample units would be missed, since 20% of the sample unit area falls outside of the crew's observing-range for metates (This assumes a random or "square" spatial distribution of metates, or other site types, with respect to the boundaries of the average sampling unit; that is, if we graphically superimposed all possible sample units with the site locations in place, we would expect to find a more or less random distribution of sites within the sample unit-shaped rectangle).

Data collected during the ARID-I fieldwork suggests quite strongly that many of the site types that characterize the area have observing-ranges that are far less than desirable given the 50 meter spacing employed. For example, I recorded a total of eleven sites which consisted of isolated, chipped-stone artifacts. In each case, I noted the approximate distance from my line of march to the location of the isolate on the ground; in no case was this distance greater than two meters. These results suggest an observing-range of less than five meters for small isolates and (using the above formula) that over 90% of all such isolates, lying within sample units, were missed during the inventory.

The validity problem inherent in using site frequency data from the sample to directly estimate total site frequencies should now be apparent. Such direct estimates can tell us approximately how many sites would be recorded if the entire project area were traversed using the same inventory technique; but they do not provide a valid estimate of the actual number of sites since the frequencies recorded per sample unit are not an accurate reflection of the actual number of sites in that sample unit.

The fact that different site types have different observing-ranges produces an additional problem in the estimation process; for it is clear that small isolates are quite difficult to observe at any distance, cairns and other supra-surface sites can be visible at considerable distances, while flake and sherd scatters seem to be of intermediate difficulty. Similarly, it may be noted that, for any given crew spacing, the larger the area covered by a site the more likely it will be observed.

Unfortunately, the problems inherent in crew spacing did not become clear until well into the course of the ARID-I fieldwork. Thus, the data that were collected in an effort to correct for this problem have proven insufficient. Accordingly, about all that can be said with any degree of certainty is that the site estimates provided in Chapter 7 should tend to underpredict the actual numbers of (surface) sites in the project area, and that this underprediction should be greatest for small, easily-overlooked sites like chipped-stone isolates.

This concludes our investigation of the validity of various aspects of the ARID-I research design. Although we have by no means examined all potential problem areas, the investigation has hit upon those which I feel are particularly germane, in terms of their impact on the overall research effort. I shall have occasion to reexamine several of these validity conclusions in Chapter 7.

The reader should now possess a working understanding of the validity concept: that validity is concerned with evaluating the "functions" of different research elements and with pin-pointing problems associated with these functions. Hopefully, this discussion has contributed to the effectiveness of ARID-I as a research and management tool, as well as to other archaeological projects, in which readers may elect to utilize the process of validity evaluation.

B. Reliability

Reliability is concerned with variability in any measurement device or other research tool. Whereas validity asks what something does, reliability examines the consistency with which it is done. Consider an extreme example.

Suppose that a foolish archaeologist elected to conduct a field inventory using standard survey techniques - with one exception: crew members would be required to keep their gaze fixed in the sky! Such an approach would be grossly invalid, since it would not lead to accurate measurements of site frequencies or other relevant phenomena. At the same time, this eye-in-the-sky method is quite reliable, since it would produce highly consistent results (i.e. a series of zeroes) in relation to the actual occurrence of the measured phenomena. Similarly, any observer could repeat the measuring procedure in the same locale and would obtain precisely the same results.

This example not only indicates the difference between validity and reliability but also points out that high reliability means comparatively little unless validity is also present. Let us examine the principal reliability problems in the ARID-I research plan.

At one time or another most of our crew members noted that it was much easier to find sites on surfaces that were smooth, fine-grained and homogeneous than on ones which were heterogeneous and irregular. It was generally agreed, for example, that bare playas provided the easiest matrix for locating sites, while heavily-dissected slopes or fans, with comparatively dense vegetation or rock-debris cover proved most difficult. Undoubtedly, these observational differences reflect navigational as well as visual problems in the more heterogeneous environments.

In general, this difference creates a serious and rather complicated reliability problem. The loss of reliability rests in the fact (actually it is an assumption, although based on experience) that our ability to find sites tends to vary with terrain, or that the proportion of the total sites that are actually observed is not consistent from sample units in one type of environment to those in another.

Under normal circumstances, a researcher may attempt to access reliability, and control for its loss, by analytical tests for covariance. In the case above, this would involve comparing site frequencies for sample units possessing different physical surfaces and identifying any significant differences. Generally, such differences could be attributed to the lack of reliability in one's measurement system and corrective steps could be taken. Unfortunately, there are also theoretical reasons for expecting (causal) relationships between site frequencies and terrain elements. Similarly, the validity analysis above has suggested that the relocation or burying of sites by environmental action may also tend to vary as a function of terrain. Thus, in this particular case, an analytically-observed relationship between site frequencies and terrain features leaves unanswered the question of which of these factors, or combination thereof, is at work.

Various situational factors, such as weather conditions, can also influence the ability to accurately and consistently observe sites. Several crew members noted, for example, that the position of the sun in relation to the line of march had an important effect on the visibility of sites; some felt that lightly overcast days were ideal in this regard. On several occasions, crews were able to complete two sample units in one day, and I have come to feel that the personal fatigue factor thus introduced may also have had an impact on reliability. It should probably also be noted that the ARID-I fieldwork covered two full desert seasons and that this may have led to subtle changes in the manner in which environmental variables were measured.

For each of these situational conditions, reliability tests are more easily conducted since there are no theoretical reasons for expecting relationships between site frequencies, on the one hand, and factors such as time of day, on the other. Although data analysis failed to reveal any noticeable impact on reliability produced by any of these factors, it should be stressed that the ARID-I sample is rather small, particularly given the number and importance of other variables, to expect very meaningful results in these tests.

Certainly one of the more serious reliability questions for ARID-I in particular and archaeological surveys in general, concerns the potential for variability in the capacities of different observers to find and record sites. Let us examine this question as it pertains to ARID-I.

In mid-December (1977), I left the field to begin the laboratory phase of ARID-I. At that time, exactly 100 sample units had been completed from the Stage I sample, and I felt that this would be an opportune point to consider the possible effect of crew composition on site recordation. For purposes of simplicity, I chose to concentrate specifically on prehistoric sites and to compare two basic crew types. These will be termed "A" and "B" crews (the labelling reflects a set of particular differences in crew composition, which I shall not identify for discretionary purposes).

The initial results of my analysis suggested a rather striking difference: through the first 100 sample units, "A" crews averaged 0.63 sites per sample unit (24 sites in 38 sample units; here and throughout the remainder of this section, sites recorded off of sample units are excluded from consideration) while "B" crews averaged only 0.13 (8 sites in 62 sample units). To examine this question in detail, I prepared the data in a manner more conducive to the generation of probability measures.

Table 6-1 contrasts a) "A" versus "B" crews; and b) sample units in which no sites were found versus sample units in which one or more sites were located. Again, the difference between the "A" and "B" crews in terms of the likelihood of observing sites is quite noticeable. "A" crews recorded sites in over 47% of their sample units, "B" crews in less than 10% of theirs. The difference is statistically significant at the 0.001 level in a Fisher's Exact Test.

While we cannot be certain that this statistical difference is a real one (i.e. that the difference would persist if both crew types were to complete an infinite number of sample units), it is useful to assume that it is and to ask why the difference exists. It is possible, for example, that each type of crew was assigned a different kind of sample unit and that the observed differences in site frequencies reflect inherent differences in the numbers of sites actually present in the different sample unit types. Since the Stage I sample units were not assigned randomly to crews, this seemed to be a rather likely possibility.

To investigate the effect of non-random sample unit assignment, sample units were partioned in accordance with the major stratifying variable, landform. The result is an expanded view of Table 6-1, in which "mountain," "valley" and "playa" sample units are distinguished. The results are shown in Table 6-2. The table indicates that regardless of the landform involved, the "A" crews maintain a consistently higher "success rate," in terms of their ability to locate sites. When the Fisher's Exact Test probabilities in Table 6-2 are pooled (this technique will be outlined in Chapter 7), we find that the probability of these combined results occurring by chance is less than 0.001.

Although by no means conclusive, this test suggests quite strongly that the differences observed between the "A" and "B" crews reflects differences in the techniques or abilities of these two crew types, rather than some external influence such as the non-random assignment of sample units. In regard to the question of technique, one point immediately comes to mind. The 50 meter spacing required of crews demanded constant head movements and changes of visual focus in an effort to visually cover as much of the inventory area as was possible. It is quite difficult, if not impossible, to standardize these observational techniques from one crew member to another in any meaningful way. In fact, it is evident from discussions with various field personnel that some crew members spent much of their time looking straight ahead while others were more inclined to scan; that some tended to fix their observations at more or less constant distances, while others chose to vary the distance of their visual focus (or course, terrain conditions and navigational problems prescribe, in part, where any crew member is able to look at any given time; this only complicates the standardization problem).

I felt that these differences in observational methods might well account for at least a portion of the recorded differences between the "A" and "B" crews. Since it was clear that most isolated artifacts were the most difficult site types to observe at any great distance, it seemed reasonable to test for differences in the relative success of "A" and "B" crews in finding isolates versus other types of (prehistoric) sites. In performing this test, I initially found that "A" crews had recorded over 80% of all isolates while completing only 38% of the first 100 sample units. This seemed to be a good indication that "A" and "B" crews differed in terms of their relative abilities to find and record disparate site types. In fact, if we partition the results in Table 6-1 to distinguish isolates from other site types, we find that the overall difference between "A" and "B" crews is concentrated largely in the former case. Table 6-3 demonstrates this result: while the difference between the two crew types for isolates is significant at the 0.01 level (using Fisher's Exact Test), the difference for other site types is not significant at the 0.05 level.

The above series of tests leads to the following set of

tentative conclusions:

1. Crew composition appears to be related to differences in site frequency counts;

2. These differences seem to be the result of differences in the abilities of crew members to identify sites and/or in the observational methods used to locate sites, rather than differences in external factors such as the non-random assignment of sample untis;

3. The differences resulting from crew composition appear magnified in the case of isolated artifacts and possibly do not even exist for other types of sites.

In conclusion, it is reasonable to assume that crew composition constitutes an important reliability problem for ARID-I. There are two basic reasons for attempting to isolate such problems. First, the information may be used as a means of eliminating the problem during the measurement phase of the research. Toward this end, at the outset of Stage II, crew chiefs were informed of the above findings and efforts were made to further standardize observational procedures. An attempt was also made to randomly assign sample units to crews, but this proved logistically infeasible and was soon abandoned. In any event, the differences with crew composition noted above all but disappeared through the remained of Stage I and all of Stage II.

Secondly, such reliability checks are also important because they provide a basis for implementing statistical controls during the analysis phase. Such controls make it possible to accurately estimate parameters such as site densities, despite existing problems in measurement reliability. The following chapter, which presents the results of the analysis, will refer again to these reliability controls.

C. Summary and Conclusions

Validity and reliability are addressed to the effectiveness of the various aspects of a research scheme. Validity is concerned with the question of what a particular research tool accomplishes, that is, whether or not each such tool does what we want it to. Invalid procedures generally lead to invalid (or erroneous) conclusions, because an effective research design demands a close correspondence between the real and ascribed functions of all components in the design. In short, research designs with invalid components are themselves invalid.

Whereas validity is concerned with what a particular measurement device or other design element does, reliability is concerned with the consistency with which this function is achieved. A research tool may be quite valid, but thoroughly unreliable, or vice versa. Reliability is constructive, however, only when high valid-

ity is similarly present. Unreliable procedures can also lead
to invalid conclusions since, for example, the former may artificially produce a record of variability in some topic phenomenon
which is attributed, theoretically speaking, to some other determining factor.

Checks for validity and reliability are important to any
research design because they force us to clarify (to ourselves
as well as to our readers) what we are doing (validity) and to
identify and control for variability introduced by our research
procedures (reliability).

Validity and reliability may take a variety of forms. All
aspects of any research plan can and should be evaluated with
respect to their validity and reliability. Obviously, this cannot
involve detailed formal or quantitative analysis in every case;
thus, in many instances it is necessary or sufficient to limit
validity/reliability testing to a careful inspection of a measurement or other tool and a thoughtful consideration of potential
problems.

In this chapter, I have attempted to introduce the concepts
of validity and reliability and to demonstrate their formal application through a discussion of specific cases drawn from ARID-I.
The examples examined above should not be interpreted to be the
total series of validity/reliability checks which should or
have been performed in this research; such an inventory could
easily fill an entire volume for broadly-oriented archaeological
projects like ARID-I. Rather the above discussion should be
viewed as a set of examples designed to provide insight to the
impact of the validity and reliability concepts and the scope of
their application. In order to increase the relevance of this
chapter to ARID-I, in particular, I have chosen examples which
strike me as being particularly critical to the interpretation of
the findings and conclusions of this research. Hopefully, this
chapter has not only served this specific end, but has also provided a basis for research that is more sensitive to validity
and reliability concerns throughout archaeology.

Note

The issue of site dislocation by environmental action leads
to another more basic problem that must be confronted. From a
purely theoretical viewpoint, the archaeologist is concerned only
with the original location of human behavior and material deposi-
tion; the environmental relocation of cultural remains thus represents only a confounding influence that should somehow be corrected
for.

From a management standpoint, however, both the original and
present loci of cultural materials are important. Present locations
are critical (even if these include museums or private collections)
since the protection of cultural resources, wherever they may be,

is a prime management concern. In this sense, it is important
only to know where the cultural resources are today and the
causes underlying their presence at these locations becomes of
minor importance. Statements about the original locations of
cultural resources (i.e. where they were first deposited) are
also valuable from a management viewpoint, however, because
the historical documentation and theoretical insights that these
statements provide should be as important to the formulation of
management decisions as are the cultural resources themselves.

It should be noted that standard archaeological survey
techniques, such as those employed in ARID-I, serve the protecting function of cultural resource management most directly, since
these techniques accurately identify the present location of
cultural remains. The theoretical and documentary dimensions of
management should not be overlooked, however. It is thus important for us to attempt to make some statements about the operation
of the environment in the relocation (and burying) of sites, as
a means of reconstructing the original locations of sites even
if such statements must be qualitative, imprecise and somewhat
speculative in nature.

In this regard, the following generalizations appear justified:

1. When dislocation occurs, resources will almost invariably be
    moved to lower, rather than higher elevations;

2. All other factors being equal, the probability and distance
    of dislocation will be a positive function of slope;

3. Heavily-eroded areas are the most likely loci for site dis-
    location.

4. In general, we would expect cultural resources to be moved
    in accordance with the typical desert erosion/deposition
    process. Thus, the likelihood of site-burying, as opposed to
    dislocation along the surface, should increase as the resources
    are found closer to the valley basin·

TABLE 6-1

THE RELATIONSHIP BETWEEN CREW
COMPOSITION AND SURVEY RESULTS

	"A" Crews	"B" Crews	
Sample units without (prehistoric) sites	20 (28.88)	56 (47.12)	76
Sample units with (prehistoric) sites	18 (9.12)	6 (14.88)	24
	38	62	100

Fisher's Exact Test: $p < 0.001$

(expected values are shown in parentheses)

TABLE 6-2

THE RELATIONSHIP BETWEEN CREW COMPOSITION
AND SURVEY RESULTS, CONTROLLING FOR
LANDFORM CATEGORY

Crew Type

	"A"	"B"	
No sites recorded	15 (20.25)	32 (26.75)	Valley Units
Sites recorded	13 (7.75)	5 (10.25)	

Fisher's Exact Test: p < 0.01

	"A"	"B"	
No sites recorded	5 (7.08)	18 (15.92)	Mountain Units
Sites recorded	3 (0.92)	0 (2.08)	

Fisher's Exact Test: p < 0.05

	"A"	"B"	
No sites recorded	0 (1.33)	6 (4.67)	Playa Units
Sites recorded	2 (0.67)	1 (2.33)	

Fisher's Exact Test: p < 0.09

(expected values shown in parentheses)

TABLE 6-3

THE EFFECT OF CREW TYPE ON
THE LOCATION OF ISOLATES

Crew Type

	"A"	"B"	
Isolates not recorded	28 (33.44)	60 (54.56)	Isolates
Isolates recorded	10 (4.56)	2 (69.44)	

Fisher's Exact Test: p < 0.001

	"A"	"B"	
Non-isolates recorded	30 (33.06)	57 (53.94)	Non-isolates
Non-isolates not recorded	8 (4.94)	5 (8.06)	

Fisher's Exact Test: p > 0.05

(expected values are shown in parentheses)

CHAPTER 7.   RESULTS

This chapter is concerned with the results of ARID-I, that is with the data analysis portion of the research and the conclusions derived from that analysis. Since this is a comparatively long chapter, it will be useful to begin by briefly outlining the topics that will be discussed.

First, I will review what I consider to be the basic objectives of the analysis phase. Secondly, the approach used to meet these objectives will be examined. Thirdly, the most important features of the raw data collected during the Inventory will be described. Fourthly, a series of site estimates for the entire ARID-I project area, extrapolated from the sample data, will be presented and discussed. Fifthly, I will outline some of the theoretical conclusions that may be derived from ARID-I on the basis of analytically-observed relationships between site location data, on the one hand, and environmental data, on the other. Finally, I will review the overall results of the analysis and make some suggestions concerning possible directions for future research, in the California Desert in general and the Northeast Mojave in particular.

A.   Objectives

I felt that there were two basic objectives for the analysis phase of ARID-I. The first consists of using the sample data on archaeological (including historical) sites, in conjunction with the stratification design and information on environmental variables, to estimate site density and locational parameters for the entire project area. Among other purposes, these results could be used for sensitivity scaling. Secondly, the analysis should seek to identify meaningful relationships between site and environmental data and to relate these, correspondingly, to specific theoretical conclusions concerning past human activity in the Northeast Mojave region.

These two objectives are subtly related. Each is concerned with where sites are located; each with the environmental matrix in which sites occur. At this point, the similarities tend to disappear. While both are concerned with sites, the latter is more directly interested in the underlying behavior which the sites signify. While the former seeks relationships between site locations and environmental variables simply to produce density and other estimates, the latter is interested in the relationships in their own right, for what they can tell us about the pattern of past human activity.

These objectives are related, however, in another, particularly important way. Extrapolations which are based exclusively on "correlations", which are insensitive to theoretical concerns,

easily overlook spurious relationships (i.e. not causal relationships) and "ghosts" created by sampling error, theoretically
oriented research can more readily discriminate the real from the
imaginary. In this sense, the second objective is integral to
and a critical aspect of the first. Thus, even studies which are
directly addressed only to the generation of site predictions must
(or should) involve themselves with an examination of the theoreti-
cally-relevant issues. The analytical plan which has been used in
ARID-I has hopefully been successful in meeting both of these inter-
related objectives.

B. Approach

The analytical strategy employed in ARID-I is built around
two fundamental conclusions. First, I determined that analysis
should be performed by the transect; that is, the analysis should
endeavor to compare the characteristics of different sample units
(in terms of site frequencies, environmental variables, etc.),
rather than other possible analytical units. I bring up this point
because the BLM inventory forms are apparently designed for analysis by the site rather than the sample unit, since the Site Survey
Form is pre-coded (i.e. they pose fixed-alternative questions),
whereas the Sample Unit Record Form requires open-ended, discursive
responses. The problem with analysis by the site is that there is
no (easy) way to control for where sites are not. Analysis by the
sample unit provides such controls since some units, of course,
contain no sites. For much the same reason, comparisons of sample
units (rather than sites) leads more directly to accurate density
and distributional estimates and to the discovery of meaningful
relationships with environmental variables.

Secondly, I recognized that the analysis must concentrate on
sites located within sample units. Sites recorded outside the
boundaries of sample units (including those recorded by other
investigators prior to ARID-I) can contribute comparatively little
to the quantitative analysis since there exists no control over
the amount of area covered per site. In fact, analysis by the
sample unit is useful, in large part, precisely because it provides
a direct measure of sites per unit area. For this reason, sites
recorded off of transects were used in only a very limited way
during the analysis.

The analysis was performed on ARI's Tandy TRS-80 microcom-
puter. This system includes an advanced BASIC programming
language, 16K of useable memory (RAM) and a cassette tape which
was used for the storage and retrieval of statistical routines
and data files. My only complaint with this particular system
for our work concerned the slow loading time for data files.
In general, we were able to develop a comparatively sophisticated package of interactive statistical and data-manipulation
routines which accomplished the necessary analytical tasks
quickly and efficiently.

Initially, the following set of routines was designed specifically for the ARID-I analysis:

1. CROSSTAB - performs the crosstabulation of data along a maximum of three dimensions (i.e. variates), providing expected and Chi Square values. This program permits the user to define and redefine the limits of variable categories at numerous points in execution.

2. REGRESSION AND CORRELATION - performs simple regression, Pearson Correlation, partial correlation, tri-variate multiple regression, bivariate plots and tests of significance (F-tests).

3. RANK ORDER CORRELATION - computes Spearman's r.

4. ANOVA (One Way) - performs one-way analysis of variance, allowing the user to define category limits for the nominal scale variable during execution.

5. ANOVA (Two Way) - performs two-way analysis of variance, for situations in which cell frequencies are unequal, using the approximation method outlined by Walker and Lev (1953: 381-82).

6. FISHER'S EXACT TEST - computes exact probabilities for 2 x 2 contingency tables. This proved an indispensable program, performing truly enormous calculations.

As I began to look more closely at the ARID-I data set (the reader should recall that preparations for the analysis preceded the completion of the Stage I fieldwork) I realized, much to my chagrin, that the Regression/Correlation and Analysis of Variance programs could not be used with the Stage I data. This followed from the discovery that site frequencies per sample unit were not normally distributed; rather, the Stage I sampling distribution has a mode of zero, a short tail of positive values and, of course, no negative values to counter-balance (see Table 7-1). Since regression, correlation and analysis of variance are built upon the assumption of normality, their use with the Stage I data would have been invalid (see Chapter 6).

The lack of normality in the topic variable also led me to another important decision concerning the orientation of the analysis. Rather than consistently discriminating sample units with one site from units with two or more sites, I decided that it would frequently be useful to pool these, thus only differentiating sample units without sites from ones with sites. Basically, this involved treating the site frequency data as a binomial distribution.

Two fundamental facts, beyond the absence of normality, prompted this binomial approach. First, if one differentiates sample units with different numbers of sites, one is making an assumption of site independence that would be difficult to sustain. There were, for example, a number of sample units in which we recorded several sites, where it would be quite difficult to determine if these sites represented the same or different occupations, recurring occupations by the same or different groups, and so on. Quite simply, the spatial proximity of such sites leads to a question of interdependence which cannot be ignored and which arbitrary site boundary criteria obviously cannot answer. The binomial approach, of course, neatly avoids the interdependence issue entirely.

Secondly, the use of the binomial makes it possible to compute exact probabilities relating, for example, to the total number of units within the total project area which possess sites. To perform these calculations, an additional statistical routine was developed by ARI. This program computes confidence limits for the mean number of "successes" (or "hits") in a population based upon a random sample of data (The terms "success" and "failure" or "hit" and "miss" are traditional and simply refer to the two possible outcomes in a binomial experiment. In treating sites per sample unit as a binomial population, our sampling procedure becomes such an experiment). The program arrives at confidence limits using: a) discrete probabilities generated from the expansion of $\binom{N}{r} p^r q^{N-r}$ (where N is the sample size, p and q are the proportions of successes and failures, respectively, in the sample, and r is the number of successes for which an exact probability is sought) and b) linear interpolation (see Clopper and Pearson 1934). In addition, the binomial approach permitted the use of Fisher's Exact Test for computing exact probabilities concerning mathematical (as opposed to causal) relationships between variables.

Given the nature of the Stage I data, its analysis rests almost exclusively on the Crosstab/Chi Square, Fisher's Exact Test and Binomial Confidence Limits routines.

A few words should also be mentioned concerning the specific variables used in the analysis. Rather than including a laundry list of environmental variables, I elected to concentrate in greater detail on a much smaller number of carefully-selected variables, which I felt might prove especially telling predictors. These included the following:

1. Vegetation
    a. distance to nearest juniper/piñon stand
    b. presence or absence of yucca/joshua in the sample unit
    c. vegetation cover, as a percent of the total surface area
    d. distance to the nearest mesquite groves

2. Geophysical
    a. distance to pediment/mountain-slope interface
    b. valley width
    c. elevation
    d. landform

3. Water Resource
    a. distance to nearest (recorded) spring
    b. distance to nearest playa
    c. distance to valley floor

4. Control variables
    a. Planning Unit
    b. crew composition
    c. block (Stage II only)

The analysis examined all site types, both individually and pooled together.

C. The Basic Data

This section briefly outlines the principal characteristics of the data collected during the ARID-I fieldwork. It is impossible of course to describe all of the data, or to present it in a fashion which is best suited for all purposes. What I have tried to do here is to select and arrange in a manner which seems generally to do the best job of providing a sound, overall view of the basic data.

We were able to chronologically place only 19 of the 159 prehistoric sites recorded during the ARID-I fieldwork. The majority of these were diagnostic tool types, found as isolates, or pottery. Given the overall predominance of undated prehistoric sites in the sample (most of the historic sites could be assigned at least approximate dates), chronology did not play a significant role in the quantitative analysis of data. Accordingly, the discussion of dated sites has been reserved for the following chapter.

One of the few uses of the "off-transect" data is as a simple reliability check on the measurement procedures used while inventorying the Stage I sample units. This check consists of a comparison of the raw frequencies (from Table 7-2) for "within-" and "off-transect", respectively, and may be performed using a rank-order correlation test such as Spearman's r (see Blalock 1960: 317-19). Basically, a high correlation would provide support for the conclusion that the relative frequencies recorded in the "within transect" column are reliable (i.e. that we would obtain approximately the same relative frequencies with another random sample in the same area). Combining prehistoric and historic sites and performing Spearman's test, we obtain a correlation value of 0.19, which is not statistically significant at the 0.05 level. However, if we examine the major discrepancies in the two sets of relative frequencies (again, see Table 7-2), a familiar pattern emerges: all of the site types which scored unusually high in the "off-transect" category (i.e. rock shelters, mines and railroad berms) are ones which stand out as being especially noticeable, even over considerable distances. These discrepancies are thus precisely the differences one would expect to find between "within-" and "off-transect" frequencies (since these specific site types are

observable at distances greater than the width of a sample unit).
This result, in itself, supports our reliability argument. And,
if we remove these three types from the calculations, Spearman's
r equals 0.65, which is significant at the 0.02 level. In general
then, these results do support the reliability of the relative
figures shown in Table 7-2.

Table 7-3 deals with prehistoric site components. It records
the numbers of sites containing each of 8 specific components.
Once again, figures for "within-" and "off-transect" are provided.
Using Spearman's r once more, we find that the rank-order correlation between the two sets of frequencies is 0.78 - a rather strong
indication of the reliability of the (relative) "within-transect"
results.

Table 7-4, which is divided into nine separate tables, records
the distribution of valley/playa transects with respect to the
principal environmental variables examined in the analysis. Within
each table, category limits have been selected so as to achieve a
more or less proportionate distribution of sample units among categories. One rather striking relationship between two of the variables, elevation and "yucca/joshua", should be mentioned. 82%
(28 of 34) of all transects in which yucca or joshua was reported
(during the fieldwork) fall between 2750 and 4000 feet elevation.
Conversely, only 9% (6 of 67) of all transects at lower or higher
elevations were reported to contain yucca or joshua. This relationship is important because these two variables prove to be important
predictors of site distributions; however, since the two are so
closely related it has proven difficult to isolate their respective
influences. Similarly, other covarying environmental facors may
be present which may also account for this site distribution pattern.
Section E of this chapter will reexamine this problem in somewhat
more detail.

Tables 7-5 through 7-8 deal with the Stage II data set. 7-5
shows the distribution of sample units by site frequency and block.
7-6 describes the distribution of sites by type and 7-7 the compon-
ential make-up of the Stage II site data. Table 7-8 reports the
distribution of Stage II sample units with respect to the major
environmental variables employed in the analysis.

D.   Site Estimates

This section presents a series of site estimates for the entire
Northeast Mojave area, based on the sample results obtained in
ARID-I. Following Rogge and Fuller (1977), an initial set of such
estimates may be derived from the formula:

$$Y = \sum_L S_L \left(A_L / a_L \right)$$

where, Y = the estimated number of sites in a given zone (the zone
        may be a sub-stratum, stratum or the total project area)

L = a given substratum (area)

S_L = the number of sites recorded within sub-stratum L, contained in the zone

A_L = the total area within sub-stratum L, and;

a_L = the area inventoried within L.

Since the Stage II sample was selected non-randomly, the computations are based exclusively on the Stage I data. The above formula yields the series of estimates shown in Table 7-9. Since these are extrapolations based on mean frequencies, they represent preliminary "best estimates" of the total archaeological potential within the ARID-I project area. However, since the sampling distributions, from which these means are derived, appear to be far from normal, the commonly-used method for establishing confidence intervals around these means may not be applied (see above). One alternative involves the reorganization of site data by use of the binomial. As discussed in Section C, above, this requires the partitioning of all sample units into two categories: those with sites ("hits") and those without ("misses").

Substituting "hits" for "sites", the above formula may be used to estimate overall "hit" and "hit-density" figures for the project area. These are shown in Table 7-10. The table provides the expected number of sample units containing sites (if all possible 1/8 x 1 mile units were inventoried) and the estimated proportion of such units which contain sites. The "proportion of hits" figures may be interpreted, for example, as estimates of the probability of finding one or more sites within a randomly-selected sample unit located in the corresponding stratum.

The binomial distribution routine described in the previous section may be applied in conjunction with these results to establish confidence limits for the overall proportion of hits. Since the sampling ratio varies from one sub-stratum to another (see Chapter 4), this interval must be determined by sampling sub-category. The results for the two largest sub-categories are shown in Table 7-11. One may expect, with 95% (statistical) confidence, that the proportion of all possible sample units which actually contain sites, lies within the ranges specified in the table (This assumes, however, that the raw data, on which these calculations are based, are accurate measures of actual site frequencies; in Chapter 6, I identified several reasons for expecting these raw data to be underestimates).

Since the sample sizes for the remaining stratification categories are quite small (see Table 4-2), it is not possible to obtain meaningful results for these categories by means of the above computations. The reader will recall from Chapter 4, however, that I was aware of this situation, but felt that useful results could be secured through statistical comparisons between the large and small sub-samples. One method for making such comparisons might be called a "Multi-Dimensional Fisher's Exact Test." Let us see what this method involves.

Consider the cross-partition (i.e. the cross-tabulation) of two dichotomous variables to be a single experiment in a series of related experiments. For each experiment in the series, the exact probability of obtaining the observed results (namely, the numerical relationship between the variables) may be determined using Fisher's Exact Test. If each experiment can be considered independent of the others, one may obtain a single probability for the series, by multiplying together probabilities for the separate experiments, since the probability of obtaining two or more specific outcomes in a series of trials is equal to the product of their respective probabilities (Walker and Lev, 1953: 16-17).

Since the ratio of sample units to total area varies from one stratification category to the next, it would be invalid to simply combine all valley sample units, for example, and compare them with all mountain units. We can make such a comparison, however, by using the technique described in the preceding paragraph to control for cross-stratifying variables.

Consider, for example, Table 7-12 which compares mountain and valley transects with respect to prehistoric sites. The table is divided into five, 2 x 2 tables, each contrasting mountain and valley sample units within a different sub-category from the two remaining stratifying variables (i.e. vegetation and water resources). The table includes all possible situations for which a direct comparison between "mountain" and "valley" is justified (One could not for example, compare "valley-mesquite" data with any mountain sub-category, since corresponding sub-categories do not exist in the sample).

The reader should note that in all of the comparisons in Table 7-12, the proportion of "hits" for valley sample units is either the same or higher than that for mountain units (Note: For tables d and e the proportions are equal; since p=1, they do not affect the pooled probability). This is essential for combining the probabilities as described above. Also, since no two tables share any sample units in common (obviously they cannot, since they come from separate sub-samples), we may treat each table as an independent experiment and combine the Fisher's Exact Test probabilities shown. This gives a pooled probability of more than 0.95 that there is a difference between the proportion of "hits" in the valley and mountain regions. Moreover, since only valley sample units contain multiple sites, one would be equally justified in concluding (with a 0.95 chance of being correct) that valley site densities tend to be greater.

If one looks more specifically at particular types of prehistoric sites, the above difference becomes even more pronounced. For example, all flake scatter sites and sites containing chipped stone artifacts or pottery are located outside of the mountainous areas, while all roasting pits were found in the mountains.

Collectively then, the evidence points not only to a rather striking difference between mountain and valley regions in terms of site density, but also to significant variation with respect to the composition of sites. This evidence will serve as a basis for differentiation during the remainder of the analysis.

Two other stratification categories stand out quite clearly as producing substantially higher sample unit "hit-frequencies." These categories are "mesquite" and "spring", respectively. Employing the procedures described for Table 7-12, the results for these categories are shown in Tables 7-13 and 7-14.

The reader should note, in examining both of these tables, that in each of the possible comparisons, the topic category (i.e. "mesquite" in 7-13 and "spring" in 7-14) leads to a higher proportion of sample units with hits than does the comparison category. Since these data are again mutually exclusive, we may combine the Fisher's Exact Test results as described above. This leads to probability values of less than 0.003 (for "mesquite") and 0.04 (for "spring") and suggests that each of these environmental zones should produce a higher proportion of unit areas containing sites.

With regard to historic sites, a single productive comparison can be made, that between sample units located near springs and those which are not. These results are provided in Table 7-15. The pooled probability (that there is not a difference between "spring" and "other water resources" sample units with respect to historic sites) is less than 0.03.

A series of concluding comments should be made concerning the above series of tests. It sould be mentioned, for example, that the results described above do not vary significantly from one planning unit to another, although obviously most of the tests could not be performed by individual Planning unit, given the patterned distribution of resources across them. Similarly, since the preceding chapter emphasized the relationship between crew composition and the identification of sites, it is important to point out that controlling for crew composition produced no noticeable effect on the above results.

While the above comparisons are the only ones that elicit statistically significant results, it is critical to make clear that this by no means implies that these are the only differences between stratification categories. Here, as well as later in the analysis, we shall find that the small sample size, when coupled with the low site frequencies recorded, severely limits the number of meaningful distinctions that can be made. In fact, given the sample size, we are probably correct in concluding that the differences observed above must be quite substantial to have been noted at all (This, however, does not logically follow; it is simply one of two exhaustive possibilities).

Finally, it is important to remind the reader that these are relative comparisons, and do not specify exact numbers in any sense. One can of course use the estimates and confidence intervals established for the two predominant stratification categories (see Tables 7-10 and 7-11) as a baseline to determine the approximate ranges for most of these other categories.

In many respects, however, the _relative_ conclusions are far more meaningful and useful, in themselves, than any specific numeric estimate that might be generated. In the preceding chapter, I identified a series of factors which I felt might significantly affect the correspondence between _actual_ and _recorded_ sites. These factors, which include terrain disruptions, adverse weather conditions, fatigue, crew composition, and spacing, should all contribute to the _under_-recording of sites (rather than leading to recorded sites which do not physically exist). Thus, there exists a whole series of reasons for expecting that the estimates provided at the beginning of this section seriously _under-estimate_ actual site frequencies. As one example, if we used A-crew results only, our estimate for the total number of _hits_ in the "valley/other vegetation/other water resources" category would be 5732, more than the total estimated number of _sites_ (see Table 7-9) for the _entire project_ area! As I suggested in Chapter 6, these numbers more accurately tell us approximately how many sites _would be recorded_ if the ARID-I field design was continued until the entire project area had been inventoried, than how many sites actually exist out there.

With these facts held in perspective, the reader whould begin to understand the value of the preceding relative comparisons. If we can assume that there is no significant interaction between the above factors and the stratification categories (Chapter 6 identifies one possible problem with this assumption in relation to terrain conditions), then the above relative comparisons are at least real and can thus be used for reaching meaningful conclusions about the project area.

One such conclusion involves the ranking of resource areas with respect to archaeological potential and sensitivity. Specifically, the above series of tests strongly suggests that, with respect to overall archaeological potential (as expressed in terms of proportion of "hits"), valley regions should be ranked higher than mountain areas and that, within these landform categories, mesquite and spring locations should be ranked higher than other areas. Obviously, if one ignored differences between sites, sensitivity projections for the project area would result in an essentially identical set of rankings. More will be said concerning archaeological potential and sensitivity in the next chapter.

One of the simplest tests that may be performed involves the question of whether there are more prehistoric sites than historic ones. This can be determined using the Sign Test (see Blalock 1960: 130-32). The test reveals that, in the Stage I sample, there are a total of seven sample units in which there are prehistoric sites but not historic sites and no units in which the reverse is true. The probability of this occurring by chance is less than

0.01, suggesting quite strongly that prehistoric sites predominate in the Northeast Mojave, particularly since only prehistoric sites occurred in multiple frequencies within sample units.

My personal field experience in the Northeast Mojave, however, does not seem to agree with the magnitude of this difference. One possible explanation for my intuitive disagreement is that historic sites tend to be larger, taller and more readily visible at considerable distances, thus leading to a higher proportion of historic sites recorded off transects. This in fact seems to be the case: 60% of all historic sites and only 38% of all prehistoric sites were recorded outside the limits of Stage I sample units. While these results are not statistically significant (p<0.17), they are certainly suggestive and do seem to support the earlier Sign Test findings.

I don't think that it would be correct, however, to stop here. I feel very strongly that many historic sites were passed over either because they seemed so "obvious" (e.g. the presently-inhabited, but historically-crucial community of Death Valley Junction was never recorded as a site, although we passed through it innumerable times), because the activity area was still in use (e.g. China Ranch), or in a few cases, because there was no clear evidence of antiquity. In general, I think that historic sites caused us considerable difficulty due to the obvious ambiguities involved in trying to differentiate between "contemporary" and "late-historic". Accordingly, I do not have nearly so much confidence in the reliability of our frequency/density estimates for historic sites.

E. Other Results

In this section, I will attempt to carry the analysis a little further, to talk not only about where sites are (or are not) but also about why they are there. Many of the results presented here have been arrived at by the testing of more or less specific hypotheses, but in some instances no such explicit hypotheses guided the analysis, and in a few cases I even found it difficult to develop, post hoc, a reasonable explanation for the particular relationship or difference in question. Since this report is intended primarily as a management tool, I thought it would be best to outline all observed relationships, to discuss and interpret them as best I could, and to allow the Bureau of Land Management personnel, as well as other readers, to accept or reject individual findings (with or without specific supporting arguments), as they considered appropriate, based on the evidence. Hopefully, this will make clear to the reader why this section is somewhat "uneven" with respect to theoretical discussions.

It is also important to note that one of the major differences between this section and the last concerns spatial controls. Since the preceding section focused on stratification categories, it was possible to produce concrete estimates for site and "hit" densities. In this section, we will be concerned, for the most part, with variables for which we do not possess exact area-coverage figures for the total project area. Accordingly, most of the relationships and differences reported below will not lead directly to further qualifications of the specific site estimates provided earlier. These results are provided nonetheless because they may make other important contributions to both planning and research in the California Desert.

The remainder of this section will be devoted to the presentation of specific research findings, starting with the analysis of the Stage I data and concluding with an examination of the Stage II results. We may begin by considering the results of the mountain portion of the inventory.

The 40 mountain transects produced a total of only seven sites (within-sample units). If one ignores the type of site involved, the overall distribution of mountain sites makes little sense; but when site type is controlled for, it becomes clear that mountain sites are actually quite patterned and locationally predictable. Three of these sites are historic and each is related to mining; two are actual mines and the third is the mining community of (Old) Ivanpah. Similarly, two historic sites were recorded in mountain areas but outside sample unit boundaries, and both of these are also mines. On this basis it would seem reasonable to conclude that historic activity in the mountain regions of the Northeast Mojave is dominated by mining.

Four mountain sample units contained prehistoric sites and these may be divided into two types. Two units contained a single, isolated grinding implement (one mano and one grinding slick) and in both cases the isolates were spatially associated with major canyons in the _____ Mountains (this and other omitted place names are listed in Appendix IV, unpublished). It is logical to expect grinding implements to be concentrated near major watercourse areas, where the generally-sparse perennial mountain vegetation is often more abundant. (Mountain areas conducive to the growth of annuals would also be likely locations for this type of site.) Whether these results suggest a greater concentration specifically in the _____ Range is less clear and may demand further investigation. It is noteworthy that Wallace (1977) recorded 41 prehistoric sites in _____ Canyon, although none of these were milling stations.

All remaining mountain prehistoric sites were isolated roasting pits or roasting pit clusters. Quite predictably (see Benton 1975) all of these were located in the agave belt at the lower edge of the juniper-piñon zone. Little variation from this pattern would be expected to result from further fieldwork.

Off-transect results agree rather well with the above findings. Of the six (off-transect) prehistoric sites recorded during Stage I, half are roasting pits (also directly associated with agave), the remaining three sites are rock shelters. As I noted in Section

B of this chapter, shelters are particularly easy to identify at considerable distances; this would seem to account for their predominance among the "off-transect" sites.

It is noteworthy that evidence of prehistoric hunting activity is limited to the rock shelter sites. Here, we typically found faunal remains, together with a variety of chipped stone tools and manufacturing debris. Two possible interpretations can be suggested. On the one hand, it might be argued that mountain hunting was comparatively limited in the Northeast Mojave; on the other, one could maintain that in the mountain areas the steep slopes and high degree of erosion combine to drastically disrupt or dislocate sites, particularly ones involving the smaller types of tools generally associated with hunting. (According to this argument, such tools are found in rock shelters because here erosion is minimized.) In general, although I feel that our site measurements are an accurate reflection of existing mountain sites, I do not believe that these sites, in turn, adequately account for the volume of prehistoric activity in these ranges.

As final comments concerning the mountain results, I might mention that we observed no evidence of prehistoric quarrying, or activity of any variety in the heart of the juniper-pinon zone. In general, quarrying of widely-available materials (e.g. chalcedony and basalt) seems to have been focused on the upper pediment areas (see below); the ARID-I sample size, of course, severely limits what can be said concerning the use of highly localized lithics. With regard to the absence of sites in the juniper-pinon, it should be stressed that very little area is involved here and thus only a few sample units were allocated to this domain. It is also important to note that most of the juniper-pinon is quite sparse and is located in very steep, almost inaccessible areas. Thus, we might expect to find the bulk of the evidence of pinon harvesting, for example, at lower elevations (or less precipitous highland locations).

All in all, there were so few sites recorded for the mountain areas that it is useless to attempt to perform a detailed quantitative analysis above and beyond the largely informal results described here and in the previous section. The evidence suggests that there are comparatively few mountain sites, that these represent a limited number of site types, and that the environmental matrices in which these various types occur are quite predictable. Unfortunately, the small number of sites recorded limits our ability to make these statements in relation to a statistical measure of probability. I suggest, however, that the results are sufficiently patterned to provide considerable support for the conclusions derived above.

The remainder of this section is concerned with sites located in the valley/playa regions. Once again, we find that the number of historic sites recorded within transects is quite limited, making quantitative analysis useless. However, we may again observe a strong pattern of distribution: All historic sites recorded in the valleys during Stage I are directly associated with principal water sources (however, see below for different results from Stage II). Here reliability (or permanence) of the source appears to be the key, since all of the sites were found in the vicinity of active springs.

In examining the distribution of prehistoric sites, it is useful to focus on individual site components (see Table 7-3). Prior to the fieldwork, I had several very basic expectations about where these various components would be found. First, I was confident, on the basis of evidence from other desert research, that valley sites would be closely associated with mesquite zones and springs. Quite obviously, these are areas in which a variety of aboriginal food resources (and water) were available in comparative abundance. It was here that I expected to find evidence of population aggregations and diverse subsistence/settlement activities. Secondly, I expected that the yucca-joshua zone would be characterized by a comparative abundance of ground stone implements, reflecting the extensive utilization, in prehistoric times, of the seeds or fruit of the Joshua and other yucca species (see, for example, Jaeger 1941: 21; Balls 1965: 46) as well as a variety of co-occurring plants (e.g. _Eriogonum_ sp., rice grass, _Hilaria_, sp., blackbrush). Other predictions were developed during the course of the fieldwork or analysis and will be detailed below.

In investigating the distribution of prehistoric site components, we might begin by first considering sites containing projectile points (including isolates themselves). As with most component types, and in support of the above argument, mesquite proves to be a major predictor of projectile point locations. Table 7-16a contrasts sample units containing mesquite from ones which do not, with respect to the recording of sites. The table describes a significant (at the 0.05 level in a Fisher's Exact Test) association between mesquite and sample units containing projectile points - projectile points are found more frequently in mesquite zones (These and subsequent results are based on the Stage I [random] sample only).

A second key predictor variable appears to be springs. Since mesquite produces a confounding effect, we cannot demonstrate statistically the relationship between projectile points and springs in isolation. However, if we combine sample units which contain mesquite with ones lying within 3 miles of a recorded spring, we observe that _all_ sites recorded in Stage I which contain projectile points are located in this pooled category. This is shown in Table 7-16b (Some readers may wish to know that this involves six, rather than four sites since, in two of the sample units, two sites containing projectile points were recorded).

In large part, the association between projectile points on the one hand and mesquite and springs on the other can probably be associated directly with actual hunting activity rather than simply manufacturing (since several of the projectile points were isolates), reflecting the relative abundance of game in these areas. Since there are no further 'projectile point sites' to account for, their analysis need go on no further. Although one certainly would not want to conclude that hunting was restricted to these areas, there is a good case for saying that it was concentrated there.

A strong association with mesquite areas also can be observed for other chipped stone artifacts (see Table 7-17a). This would seem to reflect the variety of processing and manufacturing activities taking place in the mesquite zones. A second effective predictor variable for this component type is 'yucca-joshua'. The sample units which contain one or more yucca species (approximately 1/3 of the total valley/playa sub-sample) make up 60% (6 of 10) of all sample units containing chipped stone tools. If we pool mesquite and yucca areas together (as was done for mesquite and spring zones in Table 7-16b), we obtain the results shown in Table 7-17b; all but one sample unit containing chipped stone artifacts in Stage I fall into one of these two environmental zones.

The absence of projectile points and other hunting indicators (including natural resources) suggests that the association between yucca and other chipped stone forms may reflect the prehistoric use of the latter in the preparation of basketry, clothing and other goods from the yucca. The reader should recall, however, that the yucca/joshua community falls within a rather well-defined elevation zone and is found in association with a number of plant species (see above and Chapter 2). Dr. Kristin Berry, zoologist with the BLM Desert Planning staff, has also suggested that this zone was probably richer in terms of animal population, than the creosote community, for example. One or more of these co-occurring factors may better account for the presence of blades and scrapers and other chipped stone tools within this zone.

Ground stone implements also tend to be associated with both mesquite and yucca. In fact, as Table 7-18b attests, all valley sample units which contain ground stone also contain either mesquite or at least one yucca species. The relationship between ground stone and mesquite areas is itself significant at the 0.01 level (see Table 7-18a). These results support the basic arguments presented earlier.

As one might expect, given their numbers and diversity, flake scatter sites cause the greatest difficulty in terms of developing distributional rules. Again, mesquite proves to be an important predictor (see Table 7-19a), but a number of Stage I sample units containing flake scatters remain unaccounted for. The analysis further suggests that flake scatters are randomly (more or less) distributed with respect to the yucca zone and spring locations. Statistically speaking, there is a weak association with playa locations (Table 7-19b), which becomes slightly stronger (but not statistically significant) when we control for the presence or absence of mesquite (It is my impression that this relationship is a real one and would be more evident if we could control accurately for playa shoreline locations and if the overall sample were somewhat larger). A weak relationship also suggests that flake scatters tend to be located along the upper pediment (i.e. the point of inflex at the valley/mountain interface). The upper pediment flake scatters consist principally of locally-available lithics (particularly chalcedony), indicating that at least preliminary flaking of indigenous materials may have occurred approx-

imately where they were found. Interestingly, most sample units
containing multiple flake scatters fall along the upper pediment
(see Table 7-19c). This further supports the above claim, in the
sense that indigenous materials, like chalcedony, tend to be highly
localized. This point will be reexamined when the Stage II data
are discussed.

The best statistical predictor of flake scatter locations,
after mesquite, is the percentage of vegetation cover. In general,
flake scatters tend to occur in areas with more cover (see Table
7-19d). Interestingly, the type of vegetation involved does not
seem to matter; Table 7-19e, for example, shows the relationship
between percent coverage and flake scatters when mesquite is controlled for (the reader should note that estimates of vegetation
cover were not recorded for 49 of the 100 valley sample units;
these sample units are thus excluded from this portion of the
analysis). Eric Ritter (personal communication) has suggested
that this may reflect a general relationship between site density
and total biomass. I was able to find no intervening variables
that could statistically discount this argument.

Before presenting the results from the Stage II data analysis,
it will be useful to briefly review the rationale behind the Stage
II sampling design.

Obviously the most critical feature of the Stage II design
concerns the Block Sampling strategy utilized. The reader will
recall from Chapter 4 that the Block Sampling orientation was
designed to artificially control for environmental variables in a
fashion that would not be practical using a small random sample.
Blocks were also structured in such a manner that they could be
used directly to focus on the question of how sites were distributed
with respect to valley contour (that is, in relation to the idealized valley in cross-section). I felt, partly on the basis of
evidence from the Stage I fieldwork, that sites tended to be located
either along the valley floors or along the upper pediment, and that
the intervening area tended to be comparatively void of prehistoric
sites. I argued that the former, ecotonal areas were the more favor-
able loci for prehistoric activity because they provided immediate
access to a greater number of resource zones. Since nearly 2/3 of
the Northeast Mojave region and a majority of the entire California
Desert consists of valley systems, I felt that support for the above
expectations could provide information concerning the distribution
of sites that would be widely applicable and far more meaningful,
in terms of its implications, than any results which could be
obtained through further random sampling.

I felt that there were two basic reasons for expecting to find
valley sites concentrated in these ecotonal areas. First, such
areas provided more efficient access to a greater number of resources
given their position between neighboring resource zones. This argument is consistent with the "site catchment" concept discussed by
Thomas and Bettinger (1976: 270), and is perhaps most applicable with

respect to sites located along the typical upper pediment. Secondly, I agreed with Vita-Finzi and Higgs (1971) that in some cases sites are found in ecotones because of the primary exploitation of a neighboring zone which, because of its size or other characteristics, is itself uninhabitable (or unexploitable if inhabited). This almost certainly applies to spring locations and mesquite groves, for example. It is also important to stress that I expected lithic as well as biotic resources to have played a role in this site distribution pattern. This is particularly significant along the upper pediment, where detrital outwash activity frequently produces extensive beds of various lithic materials.

The Stage II results stand in basic agreement with those from Stage I concerning the relationship between mesquite and prehistoric site locations. Combining all sample units, this relationship is shown in Table 7-20a. If the analysis is broken down by sampling block, even more information is obtained. Only three of the seven blocks in Stage II actually contain mesquite areas. If we focus specifically on these, we observe that the relationship is actually much stronger. This is shown in Table 7-20 (b,c, and d), which produces a pooled Fisher's Exact Test probability of 0.0015. These results make a very simple, but important point: If a valley actually contains mesquite, then this becomes a key determinant of site locations within that valley; if mesquite is absent, one must look elsewhere to account for site distribution patterns (other tests indicate, for example, that beyond a radius of approximately 5 miles, mesquite has no observable effect on site locations). This will become an important consideration in the next portion of the analysis.

The test of the valley-contour hypothesis deals with a single set of data, and consists of a series of related Analyses of Variance, using these data. The specific technique employed is Two-Way Analysis of Variance, using the approximation method suggested by Walker and Lev (see above) for cases involving unequal sub-class frequencies.

The data set itself is shown in Table 7-21. In the table, the columns refer to distinct valley contour locations. Each sample unit in Stage II received a "valley location number" by dividing a) the distance from the sample unit to the valley floor (i.e. that shortest distance to the main valley drainage) by b) the distance from the valley floor to the foot of the mountains, on the same side of the valley as the sample unit itself. On this basis, each sample unit was placed in one of three contour categories, using the category limits identified in Table 7-21. The category limits themselves were set so as to minimize the relative widths of the "valley floor" and "upper pediment" categories, while at the same time insuring that at least one sample unit per block would fall in each of these categories. Simply stated, sample units placed in the "0-0.3" category are those lying nearest the floors of their respective valleys, those in the "0.7-1.0" category are nearest the mountains, and those in the "0.3-0.7" category are intermediate between the mountains and the valley floor.

The rows in Table 7-21 differentiate sample units by block and, for blocks which encompass both sides of a given valley, the side of the valley. The number of entries at the intersection of a given row and column represents the number of sample units falling into that particular sub-category; the entries themselves refer to the number of prehistoric sites recorded for each sample unit. The table excludes the Ivanpah Valley Block (G), in which no sites were recorded.

The remainder of the analysis will be based on the assumption that the site frequency data are derived from a normally-distributed population. There are still a few too many zero entries and the distribution is skewed to the right, but this assumption is much more easily justified here than for the Stage I data set. In general, this is because the Stage II sample proved much more successful in locating sites. This may be attributed to sampling error in Stage I, or the non-random selection of Stage II sample units, or perhaps a little of both. I did not set up the Stage II blocks in areas which I felt to be prime locations for sites, but this seems to have been the result in several instances. In general, the substantial discrepancy between the two samples must lead one to question the validity of each. If nothing else, the Stage II results add to our growing list of reasons for expecting the site frequency and density predictions derived from the Stage I data to be under-estimates. I will permit the reader to determine how this discrepancy might affect the other conclusions reached in this chapter.

The first Analysis of Variance compared all block/side results with respect to valley contour (Since no sample units from the western side of the Chicago Valley block fell in the "0.3-0.7" contour category, this block/side was excluded from this and all other tests in which block/sides are examined individually). The results are shown in Table 7-22.

For readers unfamiliar with Two-Way Analysis of Variance, the following interpretations will prove useful:

1. The initial two "mean-square" values shown in Table 7-22, and subsequent tables, represent unbiased estimates of the population variance (i.e. the variance in site frequencies per sample unit), based upon the observed variation between category means within the factor (block/side or contour) in question. For example, the value (26.36) in the "block/side" row of the "mean square" column in 7-22 tells us how much variation there is when one compares the mean site frequencies for all of the block/sides in question.

2. The mean square value in the "interaction" row tells us what effect block/side and contour have on one another in terms of their respective relationships (if any) with the topic variable - site frequency per sample unit. Suppose that within each of the individual block/sides we found a strong relationship between contour and site frequencies - perhaps all sample units with

large numbers of sites fell in a single contour category. If this proved to be the <u>same</u> category for each block/side, we would find a low interaction mean square value: There is a relationship between contour and site frequencies and it is <u>unaffected</u> by block/side. However, if the contour category with all the high site frequencies <u>changed</u> from one block/side to another, we should expect a high interaction value: There is a strong relationship between contour and site frequencies, but the exact nature of the relationship <u>varies</u> from block to block. Simultaneously, the interaction term tells us what effect contour has on any relationship between block/side and site frequencies.

3. The mean square value in the "error" row may be interpreted as the amount of total variation that is "unexplained" by the earlier factors. If this value is quite low, it indicates that the other factors can account for most of the total variance.

4. The magnitude of the mean square values for "block-side", "contour" and "interaction" in comparison with that for "error" tells us, <u>relatively</u> <u>speaking</u>, how much of the total variation may be "explained" (numerically, of course, not necessarily causally) by that factor. The F-values shown, which are obtained by dividing the error mean square into the other mean square values may also be interpreted in this fashion. We may now consider the implications of the results shown in Table 7-22.

This first test produced significantly high F-values for "block-side", "contour" and "interaction" (see Table 7-22). This indicates that there are relationships between "block-side" and "contour" on the one hand and site frequencies on the other, and that these relationships affect one another.

The largest F-value is that for "block-side". This is a good indication that most of the total variation occurs <u>between</u> blocks - some blocks tend to have sample units with large numbers of sites recorded, others do not. The F-value for "contour" is also quite high. This indicates that from one contour category to another, we tend to find different site frequency values. The "interaction" F-value is significant but not nearly so high as the others. This suggests that the relationship between contour and site frequencies tends to change somewhat from one block-side to another, and vice versa. We may now reexamine the raw data as a means of putting these results in concrete perspective.

As the ANOVA findings suggest, some block-sides tend to have sample units with many sites, others with sample units having very few. The former is particularly evident in the case of the western side of the Middle Amargosa block. This is in many respects a unique area, containing a large number of chalcedony flake scatters and naturally occurring chalcedony. Dr. David Weide, geological consultant to ARI, has reported that this area, is famous for its chalcedony outcrops.

The data in Table 7-21 also confirm the ANOVA results concerning the patterning of sites with respect to valley contour. As the table reveals, most sites tend to occur either near the valley floor (the 0-0.3 category) or along the upper pediment (the 0.7-1.0 category). In fact, the western side of the Middle Amargosa block is one of only two cases in which any sites were recorded in the "0.3-0.7" category, and here higher site frequency counts per sample unit consistently result for the other contour categories. Coupled with the ANOVA statistics, these results thus represent significant support for the valley-contour hypothesis.

The only other block-side in which we find any sites in the "0.3-0.7" category is the eastern side of Chicago Valley. These sites are directly associated with ___ Spring and the encompassing mesquite zone which combine to produce a comparatively unique disruption in the typical valley environment within this contour category. We may reasonably expect that both the eastern Chicago Valley and western Middle Amargosa data to have contributed to the interaction noted in the ANOVA since, among other things, these represent deviations from the typical pattern for the intermediate contour category. One should also note, however, that differences between block-sides exist with respect to where sites tend to be located in the remaining contour categories - in some cases they tend to fall in the "0.3-0.7" category, for others in the "0.7-1.0" category, and sometimes in both.

One way to determine the contribution of a given category (i.e. row or column) to a set of ANOVA results is to delete that category and recompute the requisite statistics. In Table 7-23, this is done, excluding the results from the western side of the Middle Amargosa block. The reader will observe that the between-block variation is no longer statistically significant, indicating that the bulk of the original variation resulted from the unusually high site frequencies for sample units in the excluded western Middle Amargosa area. The F-value for the "contour" factor remains comparatively high and significant at the 0.001 level, further supporting the valley contour hypothesis (or at least confirming its test implication). The results further indicate that the effect of the interaction has diminished, but remains significant, in support of the interpretations suggested in the previous paragraph.

At this point it is useful to ask whether it is possible to collapse categories, along meaningful lines, as a means of further generalizing both the data set itself and the conclusions which may be derived. Since the presence of mesquite has proven to be a major determinant of site locations, one logical possibility would be to combine block-sides which contain mesquite (i.e. Chicago Valley, Pahrump Valley and Upper Amargosa Valley). Similarly, it would be appropriate to consider the two Middle Amargosa categories together. This leaves two categories, the Lower Amargosa and Valjean Valley blocks, which may also be combined.

The result of this block pooling is shown in Table 7-24 (Since blocks containing mesquite have been combined, it was possible to incorporate the previously excluded data from the western side of Chicago Valley within this pooled category). The most noticeable feature of Table 7-24 is the high F-value for the "block-type" factor. This indicates that we have been quite successful in pooling block-sides in such a manner that sample units with similar site frequencies have been placed in the same category. This should be evident from an inspection of Table 7-21.

The fact that the F-values for both the contour and interaction factors are comparatively low (but still statistically significant) in 7-24 does not mean, however, that these factors are unimportant. Rather, the results seem to be telling us that within particular block-type categories there is still a significant relationship between valley contour and site frequency, and that between block-type categories this relationship tends to vary in form. The former conclusion may be demonstrated by performing the ANOVA for block-sides within specific block-types.

Consider for example Table 7-25 which examines block-sides within the "mesquite" block-type only. The high F-value for the contour factor in relation to those for the block-side and interaction factors indicates that each block-side of this type tends to have approximately the same overall distribution of site frequencies per sample unit, that most of the variation is accounted for in terms of a relationship between contour and site frequencies and that this variation tends to be comparatively constant across different block-sides (If we isolate the eastern side of Chicago Valley and contrast it with the pooled results from all remaining mesquite block-sides, we can observe the effect of the location of _____ Spring in the former: All these F-values increase considerably, indicating that we have made a distinction which has 1] accounted for at least some of the site variation between mesquite block-sides, 2] further revealed the relationship between contour and site frequency with this type of block, and 3] accounted for a good portion of the interaction observed in Table 7-25).

Approximately the same results as those described in Table 7-25 are achieved when we contrast block-sides with the remaining two block-types. The resultant F-values for the valley contour factors for the Middle Amargosa and Valjean/Lower Amargosa tests are 99.73 and 180.00 respectively (both are significant well beyond the 0.001 level).

Finally an examination of Table 7-21 will reveal the interaction between block-type and contour suggested in Table 7-24. In the Valjean/Lower Amargosa block type, all sites fell in the upper pediment area; for the mesquite type, most sites occurred near the valley floor (with the eastern Chicago Valley as an exception, of course), while the Middle Amargosa type might be considered somewhat intermediate.

I have become somewhat concerned about having "over-analyzed" a comparatively small data set. I will therefore stop at this point and attempt to summarize what the analysis has revealed. First, the reorganization, or pooling, of block data according to major resource areas (i.e. "mesquite" versus "chalcedony deposits" versus "other") has proven quite successful in partitioning sample units with different site frequencies. This could have been anticipated from earlier portions of the analysis, particularly those emphasizing the importance of mesquite. Secondly, it has been shown that there is a strong relationship between valley contour and site locations. In general, the specific form that this relationship takes, reflects the location of resources within particular areas. The fact that most sites tend to cluster along the valley floor and upper pediment, for example, seems to reflect the relative paucity of unique resources between these zones. Correspondingly, the deviations from this pattern can be accounted for in terms of particularly evident exceptions to this resource rule (e.g. in Chicago Valley).

In summary, I would like to argue that the above conclusions are generally applicable throughout the Northeast Mojave region and perhaps much of the California Desert as well. If this proves to be the case, then the Block Sampling Design has certainly proven its worth, for the analysis suggests that if one can correctly classify a given valley region, it is possible not only to predict the relative archaeological potential of that region but also the relative distribution of prehistoric sites across that particular valley (At this point, it is important to remind the reader that block locations were not selected randomly. Thus, among other considerations, one would not want to use the results from a given block to make generalizations about that particular valley as a unit; rather one should try to classify unique cross-sections of the valley. For example, I would initially classify the northern Chicago Valley with the Valjean/Lower Amargosa block, since it contains no mesquite). Since, as I have noted before, valley regions make up a majority of the areas in both the Northeast Mojave in particular, and the California Desert, in general, these results may prove widely significant. Hopefully, subsequent research will aid in the further qualification and elucidation of the preliminary results presented here.

Comparatively little can be said concerning the Stage II results with respect to historic sites. This is not surprising in light of the variety of sites involved. A total of eight historic sites were recorded including: a structure, dump, corral, the Tidewater and Tonopah railroad berm, an isolated whiskey bottle, temporary camp site, and a pile of machine-hewn timbers. Perhaps it is useful to point out that these sites do not exhibit the degree of special patterning that we find with prehistoric sites, much less the same type of patterning (This is somewhat different from the Stage I results). In general, I would argue that the relatively random distribution of historic sites in the Northeast Mojave reflects the comparative success of 19th and 20th century

Euro-American culture in overcoming or neutralizing environmental diversity and patterning in the California Desert. I suggest that the ability to traverse desert areas with relative ease and speed and to obtain and maintain supplies of water by diverse means have proven particularly significant in this regard.

TABLE 7-1

Distribution of Sample Units (Stage I) by Number
of Prehistoric and Historic Sites

	Prehistoric Sites	Historic Sites
Number of Sites	Number of Sample Units	Number of Sample Units
0	112	132
1	20	8
2	6	0
3	2	0
More than 3	0	0
Total	140	140

Table 7-2

Numbers of Sites (Stage I) by Site Type
Within and Off Sample Units

SITE TYPE:

	Within Sample Units	Off Sample Units
Prehistoric Site Types		
Temporary Camp	6	2
Shelter-Cave	0	7
Milling Station	3	0
Lithic Scatter	12	4
Rock Alignment	0	0
Isolated Find	12	4
Cairn	1	1
Roasting Pit	2	4
Total	36	22
Historic Site Types		
Well	1	0
Railroad	0	2
Homestead	1	2
Trail	0	1
Town	2	2
Camp	1	1
Mine	0	4
Isolated Feature	1	0
Total	7	12
Grand Total	43	34

TABLE 7-3

Numbers of Sites Containing Each of 8 Prehistoric Site
Components Within and Off Sample Units (Stage I)

| | NUMBER OF SITES | |
Prehistoric Sites Containing:	Within Sample Units	Off Sample Units
Hearths - Rock Rings	9	4
Projectile Points	6	3
Other Chipped Stone Tools	13	6
Flake Scatters	21	12
Pottery	5	1
Roasting Pits	2	4
Ground Stone	7	4
Cairns	1	3

Table 7-4

Distribution of Environmental Variables Across the
Stage I Sample (Valley/Playa Units Only)

A.

Elevation (feet) Above Sea Level	Number of Sample Units
-2000	20
2000-2500	21
2500-2700	20
2700-3000	12
3000-3500	13
3500+	14

B.

Distance to Base of Nearest Mountain Range (miles)	Number of Sample Units
-1	47
1-2	31
2-5	22
5+	0

TABLE 7-4 (Cont.)

C.

Distance to Nearest Juniper/Piñon (miles)	Number of Sample Units
- 5	9
5-10	20
10-15	13
15-20	14
20-25	13
25-30	22
30-35	9
35+	0

D.

Yucca/Joshua	Number of Sample Units
Not present	66
Present	34

E.

Vegetation Cover (Percent of total ground cover)	Number of Sample Units
Not recorded	49
- 5	22
5-10	11
10-15	11
15+	7

F.

Distance to Nearest Mesquite (miles)	Number of Sample Units
- 3	21
3- 6	15
6- 9	22
9-12	22
12-18	18
18-40	2
40+	0

TABLE 7-4 (Cont.)

G.

Distance to Nearest Playa (miles)	Number of Sample Units
- 3	23
3- 6	18
6- 9	21
9-12	15
12-18	23
18+	0

H.

Distance to Nearest Recorded Spring (miles)	Number of Sample Units
- 1	13
1- 3	17
3- 5	21
5- 7	18
7-10	19
10-15	12
15+	0

I.

Distance to Valley Floor (miles)	Number of Sample Units
- 0	19
0- 1	27
1- 3	20
3- 6	21
6-15	13
15+	0

TABLE 7-5

Distribution of Sample Units by Block and
Number of Prehistoric and Historic Sites

Number of Prehistoric Sites per Sample Unit				NUMBER OF SAMPLE UNITS					
				Block					All Blocks
	A	B	C	D	E	F	G		
0	5	8	6	3	7	7	8		44
1	3	1	3	0	1	2	0		10
2	1	0	0	1	0	0	0		2
3	0	0	1	0	0	0	0		1
4	1	0	1	3	0	0	0		5
5	1	0	0	0	0	0	0		1
6	1	0	0	1	0	0	0		2
7	0	0	0	0	0	0	0		0
8	0	0	0	3	0	0	0		3
15	0	0	0	1	0	0	0		1
Total Number of Prehistoric Sites	20	1	10	59	1	2	0		93
Number of Historic Sites per Sample Unit	A	B	C	Block D	E	F	G		All Blocks
0	10	9	8	11	8	8	8		52
1	2	0	3	1	0	1	0		7
2	0	0	0	0	0	0	0		0
Total Number of Historic Sites	2	0	3	1	0	1	0		7
Grand Total	22	1	13	60	1	3	0		100

TABLE 7-6

Numbers of Sites by Site Type, Stage II

SITE TYPE:

Prehistoric Site Types	Within Sample Units	Off Sample Units
Isolated Find	24	2
Lithic Scatter	59	3
Temporary Camp	6	1
Shelter/Cave	1	1
Quarry Site	1	0
Rock Alignment	1	0
Village	1	0
Other	0	1
Total	93	8

Historic Site Types		
Corral	2	0
Homestead	0	1
Camp	0	1
Railroad	4	0
Isolated Find	1	0
Total	7	2
Grand Total	100	10

TABLE 7-7

Numbers of Sites with Each of 6 Prehistoric
Site Components, Within Sample Units (Stage II)

Prehistoric Sites Containing:	Number of Sites
Flake Scatters	63
Projectile Points	6
Other Chipped Stone Tools	34
Hearths - Rock Alignments	3
Pottery	2
Shelters	1

TABLE 7-8

Distribution of Environmental
Variables Across Stage II Sample

A. Valley Width (miles)	Number of Sample Units
- 1.25	3
1.25- 3.00	15
3.00- 4.10	5
4.10- 4.50	9
4.50- 6.10	6
6.10- 6.25	6
6.25- 7.00	8
7.00-15.60	9

B. Yucca/Joshua	Number of Sample Units
Present	59
Not present	10

C. Distance to Valley Floor (miles)	Number of Sample Units
-0	7
0-2	24
2-4	19
4-6	10
6-7	4
7-	5

D. Distance to Mesquite (miles)	Number of Sample Units
-0	8
0-2	15
2-4	8
4-6	1
6-7	1
7-	36

E. Distance to Spring (miles)	Number of Sample Units
-0	1
0-2	15
2-4	12
4-6	13
6-7	7
7-	21

TABLE 7-9

Site Frequency & Density Estimates for the Northeast
Mojave & Selected Sub-Areas*

Stratum	Estimated Number of Sites (total)	Estimated Site Density (per square mile)
PREHISTORIC SITES		
Valley	4501	2.49
Playa	155	2.76
Mountain	615	0.73
Total ARID-I	5271	1.94
Other categories of interest:		
Mesquite zones	283	6.73
Spring locations	168	3.91
Juniper/Piñon zones	78	1.95
HISTORIC SITES		
Valley/Playa	516	0.28
Mountain	377	0.45
Total ARID-I	893	0.33

*See Tables 4-1 and 4-2 for area figures used in the computations.
The stratification criteria described in Chapter 4 provide the
basic data for these estimates.

TABLE 7-10

Estimated Hit and Hit-Density
Figures for ARID-I

Stratum	Estimated Total Number of Hits (sample units with sites)	Estimated Hit Density per Square Mile (maximum = 8)	Proportion of Hits
PREHISTORIC SITES:			
Valley	3005	1.66	0.21
Playa	155	2.76	0.34
Mountain	615	0.73	0.09
Total ARID-I	3775	1.39	0.17
Other Categories of Interest:			
Mesquite zones	213	5.08	0.64
Spring locations	168	3.91	0.49
Juniper/Piñon zones	78	1.95	0.24
HISTORIC SITES:			
Valley/Playa	516	0.28	0.04
Mountain	377	0.45	0.06
Total ARID-I	893	0.33	0.04

TABLE 7-11

95% Confidence Intervals for Proportion of Hits,
By Site Classification and Stratification Category

Site Classifications	Valley Other Water Resources Other Vegetation	Mountain Other Water Resources Other Vegetation
Prehistoric Sites	p=0.21 0.11< $\underline{P}$ <0.31	p=0.08 0< $\underline{P}$ <0.22
Historic Sites	p=0.03 0< $\underline{P}$ <0.08	p=0.04 0< $\underline{P}$ <0.15

p=Sample proportion of hits

$\underline{P}$=Population proportion of his (sample units with sites)

95% Confidence limits are shown

TABLE 7-12

Distribution of Prehistoric Sites:
Valley Vs. Mountain Areas

CONTROL CATEGORY

			VALLEY	MOUNTAIN	
a)	"Other Vegetation-Other Water Resources"	No sites recorded	54	24	p=0.13
		Sites recorded	14	2	
b)	"Other Vegetation-Spring"	No sites recorded	1	2	p=0.5
		Sites recorded	2	1	
c)	"Other Vegetation-Wells"	No sites recorded	2	2	p=0.6
		Sites recorded	1	0	
d)	"Other Vegetation-Amargosa River"	No sites recorded	7	3	p=1
		Sites recorded	0	0	
e)	"Other Vegetation-Tanks"	No sites recorded	3	1	p=1
		Sites recorded	0	0	

pooled probability=0.038

TABLE 7-13

Distribution of Prehistoric Sites:
Mesquite Vs. Other Vegetation

CONTROL CATEGORY

			MESQUITE	OTHER VEGETATION	
a)	"Valley-Amargosa River"	No sites recorded	0	7	p=0.01
		Sites recorded	3	0	
b)	"Valley-Other Water Resources"	No sites recorded	2	54	p=0.55
		Sites recorded	1	14	
c)	"Playa-Other Water Resources"	No sites recorded	2	3	p=0.5
		Sites recorded	1	0	

pooled probability=0.0022

TABLE 7-14

Distribution of Prehistoric Sites:
Spring Vs. Other Water Resources

CONTROL CATEGORY

			SPRING	OTHER WATER RESOURCES	
a)	"Valley- Other Vegetation"	No Sites recorded	1	54	p=0.13
		Sites recorded	2	14	
b)	"Mountain- Other Vegetation"	No Sites recorded	2	24	p=0.29
		Sites recorded	1	2	

pooled probability=0.0377

TABLE 7-15

Distribution of Historic Sites:
Spring Vs. Other Water Resources

CONTROL CATEGORY

			SPRING	OTHER WATER RESOURCES	
a)	"Valley- Other Vegetation"	No sites recorded	2	66	p=0.12
		Sites recorded	1	2	
b)	"Mountain- Other Vegetation"	No sites recorded	2	25	p=0.20
		Sites recorded	1	1	

pooled probability=0.024

TABLE 7-16

The Distribution of Sample Units
Containing Projectile Points

	Sample Unit Contains Mesquite	No Mesquite	
A. No sites recorded	5	91	
Sites recorded	2	2	p=0.024

	Sample Units Contain Mesquite or Lie Within 3 Miles of Spring	No Mesquite or Spring	
B. No sites recorded	32	64	
Sites recorded	4	0	p=0.015

TABLE 7-17

The Distribution of Sample Units Containing
Other Chipped Stone Artifacts

	Sample Units Within 1 Mile of Mesquite	No Mesquite	
A. No sites recorded	9	81	p=0.05
Sites recorded	5	5	

	Sample Units Containing Yucca or Within 1 Mile of Mesquite	No Yucca or Mesquite	
B. No sites recorded	37	53	p<0.004
Sites recorded	9	1	

TABLE 7-19 (Cont.)

	7% Coverage or Less	More Than 7% Coverage	
D. No sites recorded	21	22	
Sites recorded	1	7	p=0.06

Sample Units Not Containing Mesquite

	7% Coverage or Less	More Than 7% Coverage	
E. No sites recorded	19	19	
Sites recorded	0	7	p< 0.02

TABLE 7-20

The Effect of Mesquite on Prehistoric
Site Locations   (Stage II Results)

	SAMPLE UNITS WITHIN 1 MILE OF MESQUITE	NO MESQUITE	
A. ALL SAMPLE UNITS			
No sites recorded	6	38	
Sites recorded	11	14	$p < 0.01$
B. CHICAGO VALLEY BLOCK			
No sites recorded	2	3	
Sites recorded	7	0	$p = 0.045$
C. PAHRUMP VALLEY BLOCK			
No sites recorded	4	4	
Sites recorded	1	0	$p = 0.555$
D. UPPER AMARGOSA BLOCK			
No sites recorded	0	6	
Sites recorded	3	2	$p = 0.0606$

TABLE 7-21

Data for Test of Valley Contour Hypothesis

NUMBER OF SITES PER SAMPLE UNIT

BLOCK-SIDE	0-0.3 "Valley Floor"	0.3-0.7 "Intermediate"	0.7-1.0 "Upper Pediment"
Chicago Valley - West	4	(none)	0,1
Chicago Valley - East	1,2,5	0,0,1,6	0,0
Pahrump Valley	0,1	0,0,0,0	0,0,0
Upper Amargosa - West	0,3	0	1,1
Upper Amargosa - East	1,4	0,0	0,0
Middle Amargosa - West	15	2,4,6	8,8
Middle Amargosa - East	0,4,4,8	0	0
Lower Amargosa	0,0,0	0,0,0	0,1
Valjean Valley	0,0,0,0	0,0,0	1,1

TABLE 7-22

Analysis of Variance: The Distribution of
Prehistoric Sites in Relation to Block and Valley Contour

FACTOR	SUM OF SQUARES	DEGREES OF FREEDOM	MEAN SQUARE (Variance estimate)	F	SIGNIFICANCE
Block-Side	184.54	7	26.36	56.9	0.001
Contour	28.54	2	14.27	30.8	0.001
Interaction	54.14	14	3.87	8.3	0.001
Error		34	0.46		

TABLE 7-23

Analysis of Variance: The Distribution of Prehistoric
Sites in Relation to Block and Valley Contour
(excluding the western side of the Middle Amargosa Block)

FACTOR	SUM OF SQUARES	DEGREES OF FREEDOM	MEAN SQUARE (Variance estimate)	F	SIGNIFICANCE
Block-Side	5.18	6	0.86	2.13	N.S.
Contour	7.83	2	3.91	9.65	0.001
Interaction	12.85	12	1.07	2.64	0.05
Error		31	0.41		

TABLE 7-24

Analysis of Variance: The Distribution of Prehistoric Sites
in Relation to Block-Type and Valley Contour

FACTOR	SUM OF SQUARES	DEGREES OF FREEDOM	MEAN SQUARE (Variance estimate)	F	SIGNIFICANCE
Block-Type	35.93	2	17.97	33.35	0.001
Contour	2.83	2	1.41	2.62	0.05
Interaction	4.56	4	1.14	2.12	0.05
Error		54	0.54		

TABLE 7-25

Analysis of Variance: The Distribution of Prehistoric
Sites in Relation to Block and Valley Contour
(blocks containing mesquite only)

FACTOR	SUM OF SQUARES	DEGREES OF FREEDOM	MEAN SQUARE (Variance estimate)	F	SIGNIFICANCE
Block-Side	2.56	3	0.85	3.79	0.05
Contour	5.66	2	2.83	12.57	0.001
Interaction	3.51	6	0.59	2.60	0.05
Error		17	0.23		

CHAPTER 8. SITE EVALUATION AND RECOMMENDATIONS

Gary Coombs and Robert H. Crabtree

The principal purpose in undertaking this report is to provide written input toward the development of a plan for the simultaneous use and protection of cultural (and other) resources within the California Desert Conservation Area. The present chapter attempts to formulate and summarize this input in the form of a series of specific recommendations. Let us begin by considering what can be said concerning specific sites recorded during the ARID-I fieldwork.

A. Interpretations

1. Historic Sites: The historic sites which we recorded can most easily be discussed when grouped by major activity.

    a. Mines and Settlements

        SBr-2962: Remnants of various buildings associated with a spring in an important mining district (Owlshead/Amargosa Planning Unit)

        SBr-2950: Residential remains near SBr-2962 (Owlshead/Amargosa Planning Unit)

        SBr-2979: A small mine and mining camp. Bottles and tin cans indicate occupation between 1900 and 1940 (Kingston Planning Unit)

        SBr-2981: "Jumbo Mine". Tunnel and mining equipment are intact and in an excellent state of preservation. Constructed in the 1930's (Kingston Planning Unit)

        SBr-2654: A manganese mine dating from the early 1900's. Building foundations and a sluiceway remain (Owlshead/Amargosa Planning Unit)

        SBr-2990: "Shadow Mountain Mine". Includes a series of sheds, a stone residence, the mine shaft and superstructure (Kingston Planning Unit)

        SBr-2973: "Copper World". An abandoned copper smelter and homestead dating back to the early 1900's (Kingston Planning Unit)

        SBr-2978: "Old Ivanpah". Mining settlement. Casebier (1976) has observed that "...much of the history of the Eastern Mojave Desert for the 1870's is centered in Ivanpah. It was the only community of any size in all that vast country throughout the decade" (Kingston Planning Unit)

SBr-2980: An abandoned mine and camp. Includes the mine tunnel, a partially-collapsed stone building, a small corral, and a trash dump. This site appears to date from the 1920's or 30's (Kingston Planning Unit)

b. Railroad: The Tidewater & Tonopah and Death Valley railroads, which operated from 1906 to 1938, played a crucial role in the history of the project area. The following recorded sites were directly associated with the railroads.

SBr-2964 (Owlshead/Amargosa Planning Unit), Iny-1586 (Bitterwater Planning Unit), Iny-2416 (Bitterwater Planning Unit), Iny-2413 (Bitterwater Planning Unit), and Iny-2455 (Bitterwater Planning Unit): The railroad berm of the main and spur lines at various points within the project area

SBr-2949: "Sperry". A collapsed adobe structure, handcar siding and well or cistern immediately adjacent to the railbed (Owlshead/Amargosa Planning Unit)

SBr-2955: "Silver Lake Station". An adobe structure and debris (lies outside the project area; Owlshead/Amargosa Planning Unit)

SBr-2957: "Valjean". A major railway station. A number of foundations are visible (Owlshead/Amargosa Planning Unit)

c. Miscellaneous Historic Sites

SBr-2956: "Renoville". An important way-station at the junction of the Old Spanish Trail and the Kingston cutoff. Concrete slab foundations and heavily-collected trash dumps are visible (Owlshead/Amargosa Planning Unit)

SBr-2983: Consists of a number of wooden planks and a 1.5" pipe, apparently used to collect water from an adjacent spring (Kingston Planning Unit)

SBr-2989: "USMM-185". An important station on the Kingston cutoff road. Several structures are presently intact. Privately owned and currently inhabited (Kingston Planning Unit)

Iny-2357: Raised gravel road and dump area. Apparently associated with Death Valley Junction. Bottles and cans suggest use from the 1920's (Bitterwater Planning Unit)

Iny-1457: Two wooden structures and a concrete foundation associated with an active spring (Bitterwater Planning Unit)

Iny-2419: A small camp site with wooden structure and trash dump. Estimated period of use, 1930's - 1940's (Bitterwater Planning Unit)

Iny-2390: A recently used livestock pen (Bitterwater Planning Unit)

Iny-2371: "China Ranch". Numerous stone buildings and extensive debris, related to mining and railroad activity from the turn of the century (Bitterwater Planning Unit)

2. Prehistoric Sites: Chapter 3 outlined a general prehistoric chronology for the project area. Seventeen of the sites recorded during the ARID-I fieldwork may be placed within this temporal framework. These are as follows (more detailed information is contained in the site and sample unit records):

a. Period I: 10000-5000 B.C.

Iny-2366: Lake Mojave point, of brown chert, associated with a small lithic scatter in desert pavement gravels on a flat-topped ridge (interfluve; Bitterwater Planning Unit)

b. Period I or II: ca. 6000-3000 B.C.

Iny-2421: Silver Lake point (variant), an isolate on a desert pavement-capped interfluve on the upper part of an alluvial fan. The item itself is made of a fine-grained rhyolite and is heavily patinated on one surface (Bitterwater Planning Unit)

c. Period II: 5000-2000 B.C.

Iny-2352: Pinto square-shouldered point, obsidian; a surface association at an extensive site adjacent to the Amargosa River. Other surface material includes vesicular basalt mortars, manos, metates, scrapers, other flake tools, hearth debris and debitage. The site appears to be a multi-component site, with considerable lateral stratigraphy (Bitterwater Planning Unit)

Iny-2372: Humboldt concave-base point, chalcedony; an isolate on a high terrace in desert pavement southeast of an old lake basin (Bitterwater Planning Unit)

Iny-1457: Pinto square-shouldered point, of chert, in an extensive lithic scatter with intermittent midden and hearth debris at an active spring adjacent to extensive mesquite groves. This is a multi-component site about 450 to 500 meters in diameter (see also Period V below; Bitterwater Planning Unit)

SBr-2963: Northern side-notched point (dated in the northern Great Basin at 7000 to 1000 B.C. [Hester, 1973]), red and blue jasper. The site is about 1.5 miles south of an active spring and consists of a series of loci with lithic scatters, hearth material, midden patches, and scattered milling implements. This site has been subjected to extensive wind and occasional flood erosion (Owlshead/Amargosa Planning Unit)

d. Period III: 2000 B.C. - A.D. 500

SBr-2965: Gypsum Cave point, basalt, an isolate, found near high sand dunes associated with a playa (Kingston Planning Unit)

e. Period IV: A.D. 500-1100

SBr-2969: Virgin Branch pottery, North Creek gray and North Creek black-on-gray (see also Period V, below). The site extends over an area about 75 m. x 150 m. with intermittent midden patches, debitage, hearth debris, manos, metates, chipped stone artifacts and late period ceramics. This site is in an extensive mesquite grove adjacent to a playa (Kingston Planning Unit)

Iny-2451: Rose Spring corner-notched point, chert, an isolate found in mesquite groves (Bitterwater Planning Unit)

f. Period V: A.D. 1100-1900

SBr-2958: Paiute brown ware observed at an extensive site with midden, lithic debris and charred bone at a spring. This site has been damaged by off-road vehicles (Owlshead/ Amargosa Planning Unit)

SBr-2966: Cottonwood triangular point, basalt, an isolate found in high dunes and mesquite groves near a playa (Kingston Planning Unit)

SBr-2969: Paiute brown ware and Parker (Lower Colorado) buff pottery. The site is also discussed under Period IV, above (Kingston Planning Unit)

SBr-2970: Paiute brown ware and two types of Lower Colorado buff ware associated, as surface material, in a scatter 30 m. x 75 m. with lithic debris, grinding implements, chipped stone tools and hearth debris. This site is in a mesquite grove about 200 m. north of SBr-2969 (see above; Kingston Planning Unit)

SBr-2971: Paiute brown ware and Parker buff pottery in a small (10 m. x 50 m.) scatter of lithic tools and debris. This site is about 500 m. north of site SBr-2969 in a mesquite grove (Kingston Planning Unit)

SBr-2993: Parker buff sherd, in a small overhang rock shelter, with chipped stone tools, bone, chipping debris and a rock wall, the midden is about 4 m. x 7 m.. This shelter is about 500 m. from a spring (Kingston Planning Unit)

Iny-2374: Paiute brown pottery, in a small rock shelter
with flake tools, debitage and hearth debris, covering an
area of about 50 square meters in front of the shelter.
The site is located in California Valley (Bitterwater
Planning Unit)

Inv-1457: Death Valley brown pottery (one sherd observed).
this site is also described under Period III, above (Bitterwater Planning Unit)

Iny-2450: Cottonwood triangular point, in a scatter of
hearth debris and lithic waste and a partially intact circle
of rocks (about 1 m. in diameter), on a mesquite covered
dune (Bitterwater Planning Unit)

Iny-2478: Paiute brown sherd in a scatter of lithic debris,
artifacts and grinding implements, near the north end of a
playa (Bitterwater Planning Unit)

B. Significance

The issue of cultural resource management is generally approached
from the "significance" perspective; that is particular sites or
resource areas are discussed and classified with respect to their
relative significance or value. For this report, we find it useful
to distinguish two basic types of significance: that relating specifically to the scientific community and that to the public in general.
In the first category we include any value that a set of cultural
resources may have to problem-oriented research, including historical
documentaries. In the second category, we include the intrinsic
value of the resources themselves, as well as their educational,
religious, sentimental or similar significance to the people of the
U.S. or any sub-group thereof (we do not wish to imply by this division, however, that scientific value is in any sense irrelevant to
the betterment of the U.S. and its citizens). Hopefully, the evaluations and recommendations presented here prove sensitive to both
of these concerns. Let us first consider what can be said concerning the research significance of the cultural resources in the Northeast Mojave region.

There have developed two basic, opposing arguments concerning
how measures of relative research significance should be constructed.
By far the most common argument has been that sites or areas should
be ranked on the basis of their relative importance to existing
regional research problems. Glassow (1977) has criticized this
approach, suggesting that it ignores future developments in archaeological techniques and changes in theoretical and substantive
interests. Alternatively, Glassow suggests that it would be more
reasonable to establish significance criteria which insured that
a representative sample of different site types be preserved.

On the surface, Glassow's scheme seems in many respects anal-
ogous to the "shotgun" approach which characterized early American

ethnography which so many anthropologists have come to criticize. On closer examination, however, one finds that, in the way he applies his approach, Glassow readily accomodates both contemporary orientations in archaeological theory and contemporary regional research foci (In part, this is because neither Spaulding's [1960] criteria, which he employs, nor his application of them are as free of contemporary constraints as Glassow insists). The key distinction that we appreciate and wish to stress is Glassow's emphasis on variety. In general, efforts to preserve a range of site types in a range of environmental settings can easily help to meet contemporary goals and at the same time carries the best chance of meeting future ones (This seems to us to be true of educational and other goals as well). The approach taken here reflects our basic agreement with this position.

It is useful, we think, to consider how the BLM objectives of "use", on the one hand, and "protection", on the other, interrelate. Unfortunately, in the California Desert they are all too often in direct opposition - that is, use implies destruction. Many desert "recreational" activities involve intentional destruction (e.g. vandalism of rock art and historic structures, collecting of "arrowheads", etc.); with others, destruction constitutes a major by-product (e.g. off-road vehicle use across unrecognized site areas).

It is evident that the Bureau of Land Management is sensitive to this undesireable relationship since the Desert Conservation Plan, as it is emerging, seems to be oriented toward the partitioning of the Desert into "use-areas", and thus attempting to regulate and "channel" desert activity by permitting extensive use (e.g. unlimited off-road vehicle travel) in areas deemed comparatively expendable, while restricting use in others. We think that it is essential that the recommendations presented here "mesh" with this land-allocation approach, in the sense that they provide insights meaningful to it. We would like to begin this process by considering what the ARID-I fieldwork and analysis can say about the nature and characteristics of the cultural resources in the Northeast Mojave.

A sample, like the one used in ARID-I, informs us about two basic aspects of the resources within the region in question. First, it provides precise information about the locations and attributes of a specific series of sites - those sites that are actually recorded during the implementation of the sample inventory. Secondly, the sample, in conjunction with its subsequent analysis, provides more general information about unrecorded sites - what the overall pattern of cultural resources looks like, how particular site types are distributed, and so on. Obviously, both of these can contribute to decisions about the use, protection, and management of cultural resources.

In addition to the specific site interpretations offered in the preceding section, the sample results themselves can serve, for example, to identify a number of districts or "cultural resource areas" in which one finds comparatively high site densities, and/ or sites which are of a unique character and are thus indispensable from a research standpoint. Ten such districts from the project area are identified in Appendix V (unpublished). Collectively, these areas stand out as warranting particular emphasis in any management plan. We want to stress, however, that these are undoubtedly not the only areas that fall into this category, since several of those listed would not have been included had it not been for the Stage II block sample, which was of course very limited in extent.

In addition to these specific findings, the data analysis has revealed a number of site distribution patterns. Repeated evidence, for example, has pointed to the importance of mesquite areas and these, in general, should receive particular attention with regard to relative sensitivity. Sites in or near these areas tend to be larger, more complex and diversified than any others within the project area.

Regions surrounding springs (up to a distance of several miles) also have been shown to exhibit somewhat higher prehistoric site densities. This may also be true of historic sites. In general, the higher expected archaeological potential around springs also should be considered in the development of any land-use plan.

It is useful to treat the mesquite and spring zones together because, even in combination, they represent only a very small fraction of the total acreage within the Northeast Mojave. This should mean that it will not prove particularly difficult to "plan-around" these areas, in the sense that they all can be more or less easily excluded from the boundaries of areas allocated for extensive use. Given the characteristics of the sites involved, their relative densities, and the comparatively small acreage involved, this seems to us to be an essential management decision. Much the same can be said for most of the specific site complexes discussed above and identified in Appendix V. In fact, these high sensitivity areas may be sufficiently small in extent to make further protection (e.g. fencing, signs, patrolling) both feasible and effective.

The analysis presented in the preceding chapter also points to other site location patterns. Among these, the following relationships stand out:

1. Between flake scatters and the upper pediment

2. Between ground stone, chipped stone (other than projectile points, apparently) and yucca

3. Between flake scatters and areas with high (i.e. > 7%) vegetation cover

4. Between prehistoric sites in general and the valley floor or upper pediment

There are three fundamental differences between these patterns and those identified earlier. First, the results strongly suggest that these patterns involve significantly lower site densities per unit area. Secondly (but less importantly), these sites tend to be relatively small and simple (nearly 100% are either small flaking areas or isolates). Finally, the areas involved are quite large; the yucca zone alone, for example, comprises at least 30% of the entire valley region in the Northeast Mojave.

In concert, these facts suggest that it would be neither practical nor particularly useful (only under the circumstances, of course) to attempt to protect all of these areas as a means of preserving the cultural resources within them. However, it would certainly be wrong to simply write these areas off, since each seems to contain its own unique pattern of cultural resources and each can thus undoubtedly provide important information about the occupation of the desert. Similarly, we feel that it would be incorrect to focus specifically on recorded sites here, since the sample is so small and the area in question is so large. Rather, it seems most appropriate to us to develop a land-allocation plan which attempted to maintain, at varying levels of preservation, samples from each of these environmental areas. We feel that the BLM Desert Planning Staff is best equipped to determine the sizes and number of these protected areas.

We think that it would also be a mistake to limit this sampling exclusively to the above areas; it should likewise include the remaining zones (e.g. mountains, open fan areas) in which still lower site densities have been recorded. We make this suggestion not only because the ARID-I Inventory leaves many questions unanswered about the overall distribution of sites but also because areas with low site densities can potentially tell us as much about the prehistoric and historic occupation of the Desert as can high density areas. It is perhaps important to point out that much past Desert research has tended to over-emphasize the highest density areas; in this sense, the low density areas may prove to be the best source of new information concerning Desert peoples.

The reader should note that we have been reluctant to differentiate between site types in our evaluation. This is due in large part to our agreement with Glassow that all sites are potentially important and to the realization that any significance ranking which led to the decision to sacrifice one type of site, in order to preserve one or more other types, would be grossly incorrect. We do feel that site type becomes critical, however, when one attempts to determine how to preserve or protect sites, and which sites to emphasize when allocating protection. This will become clear in the following paragraphs.

Since one of our major concerns is for the protection of sites, we suggest that it is useful to attempt to classify sites according to the relative potential for destruction or vandalism. The following criteria seem particularly germane:

1. Accessibility: In the Northeast Mojave, at least, contemporary activity seems to be limited almost exclusively to existing roads and trails and their immediate environs. Comparatively inaccessible sites thus seem to be naturally protected, at least for the moment, and thus require less imposed protection. Mountain sites, in particular, tend to fall into this category.

2. Familiarity: Clearly, some sites or artifacts are more easily recognized by the general public than others (In the _____ Springs area, for example, we met a middle-aged couple who were searching for "arrowheads". They told us that they had heard that this was a choice location. Not surprisingly, in this area we recorded a large number of crude bifaces and other tools, but very few projectile points; recognizable artifacts had been looted, unfamiliar ones remained intact). Since collecting and the looting of dump sites have become widespread "hobbies" and because vandalism continues to be a problem, familiarity is a crucial concern.

3. Value: The value of the artifact to the collector is also important. This is perhaps clearest in the case of historic sites. Dumps, for example, are selectively looted on the basis of value, either to the collector himself or in the collector's market. Clearly, sites containing familiar materials and ones which are of significant value should be afforded relatively greater protection.

4. Delicacy: Delicacy refers to the overall vulnerability of a site to destruction. Here, we are concerned with the ease with which the information contained in a site may be disrupted. This may involve intentional or unintentional human intrusions, as well as environmental disruptions. In general, the more complex or structured a site is, the more delicate it will be. Isolated artifacts, for example, represent the least delicate type of site, deep middens the most delicate.

   The criterion of delicacy brings up an important issue that we think should be considered. There are, of course, two basic ways of preserving a site. The first involves leaving it intact and protecting it as best as possible. The alternative is to remove the site and place it in a collection. We bring up this point here because sites which are not delicate are ones in which very little, if any, information is lost when the site is removed, provided of course that its precise provenience is recorded. Given the indelicacy of isolates, in particular, we would strongly recommend that the BLM consider collecting them as they are found. We are now convinced that leaving isolates in the field is all but insuring that any further information they may provide to archaeology will be lost forever. Obviously, this will be particularly true of projectile points and other familiar, valued artifacts. Conversely, more complex sites should not be collected unless necessary, since even the most careful surface collection or excavation can destroy a considerable amount of information.

Before any collection of prehistoric sites occurs, however, it would be important to confer with the appropriate Native American groups. This also may be called for with regard to certain historic sites and other American groups or individuals. This consideration reminds us that anthropologists and historians are not alone in their interest in and concern for the cultural resources of the Desert. Let us now examine what can be said concerning alternative uses of these resources.

Earlier we indicated that in general there is an inverse relationship between the protection of Desert resources, on the one hand, and the use of the Desert by the general public, on the other. It is important here to emphasize that this need not be the case - that protection and enjoyment can proceed hand in hand. When we ponder this possibility, we immediately think of the educational value to the general public of selecting a series of noteworthy sites, documenting their history and importance through informative signs or other means, and providing for their protection with ranger patrols, fencing and so on. We are convinced that with the right type of site and the proper written documentation, most members of the general public would be self-regulating in so far as preservation is concerned. Selected sections of the Tidewater & Tonopah Railroad, accessible rock shelters and pictograph sites, and several of the mining-related historic sites stand out as particularly feasible and potentially quite valuable in this regard.

It is our general impression that at the present time, the Northeast Mojave is grossly under-managed with respect to its cultural resources. This is at least in part a result of inadequate federal funding. On visiting the Northeast Mojave, one's immediate impression is that the indigenous resources are not valued by its custodians and that the area is "open for the taking". We are convinced that any efforts toward informing the general public of the value and importance of the area's cultural resources would go a long way toward helping to insure their non-destructive use and enjoyment.

C. Native American Evaluations

Richard Arnold, an informal leader of the "Pahrump Tribe", was employed as a consultant by Archaeological Research, Inc. to obtain Native American sentiments and other input regarding prehistoric cultural resources in the Northeast Mojave. Mr. Arnold interviewed 20 members of the "Pahrump Tribe", ranging in age from 25 to over 80. These individuals presently reside in Pahrump, Ash Meadows and Las Vegas, Nevada, and Shoshone and Tecopa, California. The following responses were obtained concerning the protection and preservation of prehistoric sites.

Nine of the informants indicated that "all" sites should be protected, the remainder emphasized rock art (9), cemeteries (3), milling stations (3), roasting pits (2), and "sacred places" (2).

Eleven felt that some kind of marker or monument should be placed at known Indian sites, although most were reluctant to identify site locations known to them (Locational data obtained from our Native American informants are recorded in Appendix IV, unpublished). Five suggested that known sites should be fenced. All agreed that the destruction of any prehistoric site should not be permitted.

D. Summary and Conclusions

In this chapter we have attempted to present a series of evaluations and recommendations concerning the management of the cultural resources in the Northeast Mojave. In particular, the following suggestions have been made:

1. A series of specific sites and regional complexes have been identified as particularly important and significant, in terms of their uniqueness within the project area and/or the overall high density of sites within the defined areas.

2. The relative significance of other specific sites or site types has not been offered. As we have indicated above, this is partly because we wish to avoid inferences that one site type is consistently more useful, for research or any purpose, than some other type. In addition, we feel that the analytical results which predict relative site densities within different environmental zones is, in most cases, ultimately a more useful approach for determining the allocation of use-areas than is a consideration of the ascribed significance of particular sites. The fact that the ARID-I sample size was so small should sell this argument quite convincingly, since our report can speak specifically about only a very small fraction of the total number of sites in the Northeast Mojave. The instances in which we deviate from this course are unique, usually because of the site density and/or complexity of the areas in question. Beyond these special areas, given the small sample size and paucity of recorded sites, it seems most appropriate, almost essential, to use environmental variables as a key for ensuring representative samples of all principal site types.

3. Appendix VI (unpublished) of this report consists of the Site Evaluation. The direction that this evaluation takes reflects the arguments and the approach presented here. The following features characterize the Site Evaluation:

    a. No ranking of specific sites is attempted, with the following execeptions:

        1) Zon. Sites lying within the special "zones" discussed above are identified by this label.

        2) Cpx. This designation is applied to "complex" sites (e.g. middens and extensive, structured surface sites)

which may be expected to yield proportionately greater
information concerning past human activity in the Desert.

b.   Sites are also classified with respect to the criteria of
"delicacy", "accessibility", "value", and "familiarity" detailed above. Sites which are judged particularly significant with respect to these criteria received the following
labels:

1)   Del.

2)   Acc.

3)   Val.

4)   Fam.

c.   Sites which appeared particularly vulnerable to destruction
are also identified. The following labels, with the corresponding mode of destruction, were employed:

1)   Van. Vandalism

2)   Det. Deterioration (usually applied to historic structures)

3)   Ero. Erosion (including all environmental disruptions)

4)   Act. Recent human activity that is not manifestly and
intentionally destructive (e.g. construction)

5)   Orv. Off-road vehicles

d.   Finally, sites were classified according to how we feel they
would best be protected or the information contained within
them best preserved.

1)   Col. Isolates and similar sites receive this designation, reflecting our recommendation that such sites
can best be preserved by actual collection.

2)   Ret. For many sites, such as small flake scatters, it
may not prove particularly useful to actually collect
the materials at the site, yet it may prove relatively
easy to "retrieve" the bulk of the archaeological or
historical information contained in the site, within a
few hours.

3)   Prt. this label is applied to sites which cannot be
collected or their information retrieved without excavation or other extensive fieldwork (The label stands for
"protect"). These sites usually fall into the "Cpx"
category.

4. Our final recommendation we have reserved until the conclusion of this chapter because it is, we think, a particularly important one. It is that management decisions affecting the future of the cultural resources in the Northeast Mojave, relative to the cultural resources in other Desert areas, should be made only with considerable caution.

We have tried in this report to identify as many potential problems with the ARID-I data as we possibly could. We did this because we wanted to insure that the readers of this report, particularly those who would make management decisons based upon it, would be informed readers. Repeatedly our efforts have pointed to problems that create difficulties in making one-to-one comparisons between ARID-I and other, related research projects. The different approaches which have been used in sampling, field implementation, and data analysis make this a risky business at best. Under no circumstances, for example, should the site density estimates produced here be used in making planning decisions affecting the Northeast Mojave or any other area as a whole. Alternatively, relative management decisions within the ARID-I project area can be made with considerably greater certainty because of the constancy of method and the validity of the comparative analysis that has been conducted.

In short, we would hope that planning decisions affecting the cultural resources of the Northeast Mojave will be based almost exclusively on the evidence from this area. This recommendation applies to other areas examined in a distinct fashion.

REFERENCES

Automobile Club of Southern California
  1912 Principal Automobile Roads of California. Touring Bureau
        Route and Map Service, Automobile Club of Southern California,
        Los Angeles,

Bailey, Harry D.
  1966 Lt. Sylvester Mowry's report on his march in 1855: from
        Salt Lake City to Fort Tejon. Arizona and the West 7:
        329-346.

Balls, Edward K.
  1965 Early Uses of California Plants. University of California
        Press, Berkeley.

Barth, Fredrik
  1961 Nomads of South Persia. Little-Brown, Boston.

Belden, L. Burr
  1957 Little visited county area rich in history. History in the
        Making Series, San Bernardino Sun-Telegram. February 3rd,
        p. 20.

Benson, Lyman
  1957 Plant Classification. D.C. Heath & Co., Boston.

Benton, James
  1975 Agave Roasting Pits. Manuscript on file with the Mojave
        River Valley Museum, Barstow, California.

Bettinger, Rober L.
  1977a Predicting the archaeological potential of the Inyo-Mono
         region of eastern California. In Conservation Archaeology,
         edited by Michael B. Schiffer and George J. Gumerman, pp.
         217-225. Academic Press, New York.

  1977b The surface archaeology of the Long Valley Caldera, Mono
         County, California. Archaeological Research Unit Monograph,
         No. 1. University of California, Riverside.

Blalock, Hubert M.
  1960 Social Statistics. McGraw-Hill, New York.

Blanc, Robert P. and George B. Cleveland
  1961 Pleistocene lakes of Southern California - 1. Mineral
        Information Service 14(4): 1-8. State of California,
        Division of Mines, Sacramento.

Bradley, W. Glen and James E. Deacon
  1961 The biotic communities of southern Nevada. In Pleistocene
        Studies in Southern Nevada, Part 4, pp. 201-295. Nevada
        State Museum Anthropological Papers, No. 13. Carson City.

Brainerd, George W.
  1953 A re-examination of the dating evidences for the Lake
        Mohave artifact assemblage. American Antiquity 18:
        270-271.

Campbell, E.W.C. and W.H. Campbell
  1935 The Pinto Basin Site. Southwest Museum Papers, No. 9.
        Los Angeles.

Campbell, E.W.C. et al.
  1937 The archeology of Pleistocene Lake Mohave. Southwest
        Museum Papers, No. 11. Los Angeles.

Carvalho, Solomon Nunes
  1857 Incidents of Travel and Adventure in the Far West with
        Colonel Fremont's Last Expedition Across the Rocky Mountains.
        Derby and Jackson, New York.

Casebier, Dennis G.
  1972 Carleton's Pah-Ute campaign. Tales of the Mojave Road
        Series, No. 1. Dennis G. Casebier, Publisher. Norco,
        California.

  1974 Notes pertaining to Salt Springs. Unpublished manuscript
        on file with the Bureau of Land Management, Desert Planning
        Staff, Riverside, California.

  1976 Historical Sketch of the East Mojave Planning Unit. In
        Background to Historic and Prehistoric Resources of the
        East Mojave Desert Region, Part 2, pp. 277-363. United
        States Department of the Interior, Bureau of Land Manage-
        ment, Riverside, California.

Clawson, Marion
  1971 The Bureau of Land Management. Praeger, New York.

Clewlow, C.W. Jr., R.F. Heizer and R. Berger
  1970 An assessment of radiocarbon dates for the Rose Spring Site
        (CA-INY-372), Inyo County, California. Contributions of
        the Archaeological Research Facility 7: 19-27. University
        of California, Berkeley.

Clopper, C.J. and E.S. Pearson
  1934 The use of confidence or fiducial limits illustrated in the
        case of the binomial. Biometrika 26: 404-413.

Crabtree, Robert H., Raymond J. Rodrigues and R.H. Brooks
   1970 Interim Archaeological Report on the Red Rock Area, Clark
         County, Nevada. Nevada Archaeological Survey, Desert
         Research Institute, University of Nevada, Las Vegas.

Davis, E.L.
   1963 The desert culture of the western Great Basin: a lifeway
         of seasonal transhumance. American Antiquity 29: 202-212.

Douglass, William A. and Jon Bilbao
   1975 Amerikanuak. University of Nevada Press, Reno.

Fenneman, Nevin
   1931 Physiography of the Western United States. McGraw-Hill,
         New York.

Fisher, A.K. et al.
   1893 The Death Valley Expedition, Part II. United States
         Department of Agriculture Publications, No. 7. Government
         Printing Office, Washington, D.C.

Fremont, John Charles
   1851 Report of the Exploring Expedition to the Rocky Mountains
         in the Years 1841, 1842, and to Oregon and North California
         in the Years 1843-1844. Derby Co., Buffalo, New York.

Gearhart, Patricia L.
   1974 Shoshone shelter cave number two, a preliminary report.
         Pacific Coast Archaeological Society Quarterly 10(2):
         35-50.

Glassow, Michael A.
   1977 Issues in evaluating the significance of archaeological
         resources. American Antiquity 79: 413-420.

Glennan, William S.
   1974 The Baker Site (SBr-541), an early lithic assemblage from
         the Mojave Desert. Pacific Coast Archaeological Society
         Quarterly 10(2): 17-34.

Grant, Campbell, James W. Baird and J. Kenneth Pringle
   1968 Rock drawings of the Coso Range, Inyo County California.
         Maturango Museum Publication, No. 4.

Harrington, M.R.
   1957 A Pinto Site at Little Lake, California. Southwest Museum
         Papers, No. 17, Los Angeles.

Heizer, R.F.
   1965 Problems in dating Lake Mojave artifacts. Masterkey 39(4):
         125-134. Southwest Museum, Los Angeles.

Heizer, R.F. and Rainer Berger
  1970 Radiocarbon age of Gypsum Cave culture. Contributions of
        the Archaeological Research Facility 7: 13-18. University
        of California, Berkeley.

Hester, T.R.
  1973 Chronological Ordering of Great Basin prehistory. Contribu-
        tions of the Archaeological Research Facility, No. 17.
        University of California, Berkeley.

Hester, T.R. and R.F. Heizer
  1973 Review and Discussion of Great Basin Projectile Points:
        Forms and Chronology. Archaeological Research Facility,
        University of California, Berkeley.

Hillebrand, Timothy S.
  1972 The Archaeology of the Coso Locality of the Northern Mojave
        Desert Region, California. Unpublished Ph.D. dissertation,
        University of California, Santa Barbara.

Hubbs, C., G.S. Bien and H.E. Seuss
  1965 La Jolla Natural radiocarbon measurements. Radiocarbon
        7: 66-117.

Hunt, Alice P.
  1960 Archeology of the Death Valley salt pan, California.
        University of Utah Anthropological Publications, No. 47.

Ingersoll's Century Annals of San Bernardino County, 1769 to 1904.
  1904 Ingersoll, Los Angeles.

Jaeger, Edmund C.
  1941 Desert Wild Flowers. Stanford University Press, Palo Alto.

  1957 The North American Deserts. Stanford University Press,
        Palo Alto.

Jaeger, Edmund C. and Arthur C. Smith
  1971 Introduction to the Natural History of Southern California.
        Stanford University Press, Palo Alto.

Jennings, C.W. (Compiler)
  1961 Geologic Map of California, Trona Sheet. California Division
        of Mines.

Jennings, C.W., J.L. Burnett and Bennie W. Troxel (Compilers)
  1963 Geologic Map of California, Trona Sheet. California Division
        of Mines.

Kerlinger, Fred N.
  1964 Foundations of Behavioral Research. Holt, Rinehart and
        Winston, New York.

King, Joseph
  1975 Ethnobotanical study. In Prehistoric and Historic Research
        Along the Navajo-McCullough Transmission Line Right-of-Way,
        edited by Richard H. Brook et al., pp. 10-21. Nevada Arch-
        aeological Survey, University of Nevada, Las Vegas.

Knight, Lavina C.
  1973 A figurine from China Ranch. Pacific Coast Archaeological
        Society Quarterly 9(3): 48-51.

Lanning, E.P.
  1963 Archaeology of the Rose Spring Site INY 372. University of
        California Publications in American Archaeology and Ethnology
        49(3): 237-336.

Lee, Richard B.
  1969 !Kung Bushman subsistence: an input-output analysis. In
        Environment and Cultural Behavior, edited by Andrew P. Vayda,
        pp. 47-89. Natural History Press, Garden City.

Long, Margaret
  1941 The Shadow of the Arrow. Caxton Printers, Caldwell Idaho.
        (revised 1950)

Los Angeles Star
  1861 April 13th

MacDonald, Angus A.
  1970 The Northern Mojave Desert's Little Sahara. Mineral Infor-
        mation Service 23(1): 3-6. California Division of Mines and
        Geology.

McKinney, Aileen with Duane Hafner and Jane Gothold
  1971 A report on the China Ranch area. Pacific Coast Archaeolog-
        ical Society Quarterly 7(2): 1-47.

Mehringer, Peter J., Jr.
  1967 Pollen analysis of the Tule Springs area, Nevada. Nevada
        State Museum Anthropological Papers 13(3):129-200,

Meigs, Oeveril
  1957 Weather and climate. In The North American Deserts, edited
        by Edmund C. Jaeger, pp. 13-52. Stanford University Press,
        Palo Alto.

Mendenhall, Walter C.
  1909 Some desert watering places in southeastern California and
        southwestern Nevada. United States Geological Survey Water-
        Supply Paper, No. 224. Government Printing Office, Washing-
        ton, D.C.

Mohahve
 1963-64 Victor Valley College, Victorville, California.

Morrison, Roger B.
 1965 Quarternary geology of the Great Basin. In The Quarternary of the United States, VII Congress of the International Association for Quarternary Research, edited by H.E. Wright and David G. Frey, pp. 265-285.

Munz, Philip A.
 1962 California Desert Wildflowers. University of California Press, Berkeley.

Munz, Philip A. and David Keck
 1968 A California Flora. University of California Press, Berkeley.

Myrick, David F.
 1963 Railroads of Nevada and Eastern California. Volume 2: The Southern Roads. Howell-North Books, Berkeley.

Nevada, Census of 1870
 1870 Pah-Ute County Census.

Paher, Stanley W.
 1971 Las Vegas, As It Began -- As It Grew. Nevada Publications, Las Vegas.

Rogers, Malcolm J.
 1929 Report of an archaeological reconnaissance in the Mohave Sink region. Archaeology, No. 1. San Diego Museum of Man, San Diego.

 1939 Early lithic industries of the Lower Basin of the Colorado River and adjacent desert areas. San Diego Museum Papers, No. 3.

 1945 An outline of Yuman prehistory. Southwestern Journal of Anthropology 1: 167-198.

 1966 Ancient Hunters of the Far West. Edited by R.F. Pourade. Copley Books, San Diego.

Rogge, A.E. and Steven L. Fuller.
 1977 Probabilistic survey sampling: making parameter estimates. In Conservation Archaeology, edited by Michael B. Schiffer and George J. Gumerman, pp. 227-238. Academic Press, New York.

Rosenthal, R.
 1966 Experimenter Effects in Behavioral Research. Appleton-Century-Crofts, New York.

San Bernardino Weekly Times
  1877 Supplement, February 17th

Schroeder, Albert H.
  1961 The archaeological excavations at Willow Beach, Arizona,
        1950. University of Utah Anthropological Papers, No. 50.
        Salt Lake City.

Schwartz, Douglas A., Arthur L. Lange and Raymond de Saussure
  1958 Split twig figurines in the Grand Canyon. American
        Antiquity 28: 264-274.

Shutler, Richard, Jr.
  1961 Lost City, Pueblo Grande de Nevada. Nevada State Museum
        Anthropological Papers, No. 5.

  1967 Cultural chronology in southern Nevada. Nevada State
        Museum Anthropological Papers 13: 303-308.

Shutler, Richard, Jr. and M.E. Shutler
  1962 Archaeological Survey in southern Nevada. Nevada State
        Museum Anthropological Papers, No. 7.

Shutler, Richard, Jr., M.E. Shutler and J.S. Griffith
  1960 Stuart Rockshelter, a stratified site in southern Nevada.
        Nevada State Museum Anthropological Papers, No. 3.

Smith, Gerald A.
  1963 Archaeological Survey of the Mojave River Area and Adjacent
        Regions. San Bernardino County Museum Association, San
        Bernardino, California.

  1974 Cattle Brands. San Bernardino County Museum Association,
        San Bernardino, California.

Smith, Gerald A. et al.
  1957 Archaeology of Newberry Cave, San Bernardino County,
        California. San Bernardino County Museum Association,
        Scientific Series, No. 1. San Bernardino, California.

Spaulding, Albert C.
  1960 The dimensions of archaeology. In Essays in the Science
        of Culture in Honor of Leslie A. White, edited by G.E. Dole
        and R.L. Carneiro, pp. 437-456. Crowell, New York.

Stretch, R.H.
  1867 Journal of Explorations in southern Nevada in the Spring of
        1866 by his Excellency Governor Blasdel, of Nevada. Journal
        of Nevada Senate, Third Session (1867), Appendix "E", pp.
        141-146.

Susia, Margaret L.
  1964 Tule Springs archaeological surface survey. *Nevada State Museum Anthropological Papers*, No. 12, Carson City.

Thomas, David Hurst and Robert L. Bettinger
  1976 Prehistoric piñon ecotone settlements of the Upper Reese River Valley, central Nevada. *Anthropological Papers of the American Museum of Natural History*, Volume 53, Part 3, New York.

Thompson, David G.
  1929 The Mohave Desert region, California. *United States Geological Survey Water-Supply Paper*, No. 578. Government Printing Office, Washington, D.C.

Vita-Finzi, C. and E. Higgs
  1971 Prehistoric economy in the Mount Carmel area of Palestine: site catchment analysis. *Proceedings of the Prehistoric Society* 36: 1-37.

Walker, H.M. and J. Lev
  1953 *Statistical Inference*. Holt, Rinehart and Winston, New York.

Wallace, William J.
  1962 Prehistoric cultural development in the Southern California deserts. *American Antiquity* 28: 172-180.

  1977 *Death Valley National Monument's Prehistoric Past: An Archaeological Overview*. National Park Service, Western Archaeological Center, Tucson, Arizona.

Warren, Claude N.
  1967 The San Dieguito complex: a review and hypothesis. *American Antiquity* 32: 168-185.

  1970 Time and topography: Elizabeth W.C. Campbell's approach to the prehistory of the Californian deserts. *Masterkey* 44(1): 5-14. Southwest Museum, Los Angeles.

Warren, Claude N. and Robert H. Crabtree
  In Press The prehistory of the southwestern Great Basin. *Handbook of North American Indians*. Smithsonian Institution Washington, D.C.

Warren Claude N. and Anthony J. Ranere
  1968 Outside Danger Cave: a view of Early Man in the Great Basin. Eastern New Mexico University, *Contributions in Anthropology* 1(4): 6-18.

Warren, Claude N. and D.L. True
  1961 The San Dieguito complex and its place in California prehistory. *University of California, Los Angeles, Archaeological Survey, Annual Report* 1960-61: 246-338. Los Angeles.

Warren, Elizabeth von Till
1974   Armijo's Trace Revisited: A New Interpretation of the
        Impact of the Antonio Armijo Route of 1829-1830 on the
        Development of the Old Spanish Trail. Unpublished M.A.
        thesis, University of Nevada, Las Vegas.

Warren, Elizabeth von Till and Ralph J. Roske
1978   Cultural Resources of the California Desert, 1776-1880:
        Historic Trails and Wagon Roads. Unpublished report on
        file, United States Bureau of Land Management, Desert
        Planning Unit, Riverside, California. Contract No. YA-510-
        Ph7-47, January 9th.

Westergaard, Waldemar (Editor)
1923   Diary of Dr. Thomas Flint, California to Maine and return,
        1851-1855. Historical Society of Southern California,
        Annual Publication 12(3): 53-127.

Whitney, J.D.
1865   Geological Survey of California. Geology, Report of
        Progress and Synopsis of the Field Work, from 1860 to 1864,
        pp. 469-479, Legislature of California. Caxton Press of
        Sherman & Co., Philadelphia.

Williamson, Lt. Robert S.
1856   Report of Expeditions in California for Railroad Routes
        to Connect with the Routes over the 35th and 32nd Parallels
        of North Latitude, in House Document No. 129, 33rd Congress,
        1st Session. Government Printing Office, Washington, D.C.

Worman, Frederick C.V.
1969   Archaeological Investigations at the U.S. Atomic Energy
        Commission's Nevada Test Site and Nuclear Rocket Develop-
        ment Station. Los Alamos Scientific Laboratory of the
        University of California, Los Alamos, New Mexico.

Wright, Lauren A.
1974   Geologic map of the region of central and southern Death
        Valley, eastern California and southwestern Nevada. In
        Guidebook: Death Valley Region, California and Nevada.
        70th Annual Meeting of the Cordilleran Section of the
        Geological Society of America.

APPENDIX I

BLM SITE CLASSIFICATION SYSTEM

A. ARCHAEOLOGICAL SITE TYPES. An archaeological site is defined as a locus of prehistoric activities which can be delineated specifically by the cultural remains present and can be separated by distance and/or observable geomorphic features from other loci of prehistoric activities (Historic sites are covered elsewhere). The cultural materials that constitute a site are basically artifacts and/or cultural features. Artifacts are objects manufactured or modified by man, such as projectile points, manos, metates, bone awls, etc. Cultural features are specific clusters of artifacts and/or other material used or assembled by man that exhibit structural association and that consist of nonrecoverable or composite matrices. Examples of cultural features are burials, roasting pits, bedrock mortars, pictographs, etc. The smallest spatial unit with which the archaeologist deals is the site. Therefore, a single artifact by itself, found with no other cultural material, becomes an archaeological site. Similarly, an isolated cultural feature (e.g., roasting pit) becomes an archaeological site. Most archaeological sites are made up of a cluster of artifacts or a cluster of artifacts with an associated cultural feature(s). This is illustrated as follows:

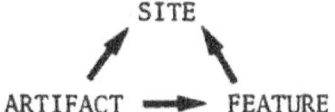

For planning purposes and to facilitate discussion of prehistoric behavior within the study area, 17 site types and 8 sub-types have been designated. Although initially developed to assist other Bureau specialists and Bureau management in understanding the variety of aboriginal activities manifested in the archaeological record, the archaeological site types used here have also turned out to be useful to the archaeologist working with the available data. They provide the archaeologist with a general category in which to place each site presently in the existing record. Obviously not all the sites will fit neatly into one or another of the site types but it does provide a means to begin dealing with the diversity in the archaeological record.

The site type given each archaeological site is determined by the information provided on the site record sheet. The existing site record sheets are limited in the amount of information they can provide. The site type given is the most accurate judgement that can be made based on the information available. The site types are flexible enough so that if additional information becomes available then the site type(s) can be changed if change is warranted.

Each site type has been given a descriptive name in order to make recognition easier and, on an extremely generalized level, to function as an activity indicator. The 17 archaeological site types and 8 sub-types are described as follows:

01 Village - This site type represents long-term or seasonal activity, usually identified as a village or base camp. A village would be identified archaeologically by primary and secondary tools (that is, tools used in the manufacture of other tools) and a variety of other artifacts, as well as floral and faunal remains which represented subsistence activities. Such a site would be characterized by extensive scatters and quantities of debris such as potsherds, fire-affected rock, whole and broken flaked stone tools, chipping waste, charred bone, milling tools, house structures, hearths, rock rings, and sometimes rock art or burials and cremations. A well developed midden is usually a component of this site type.

02 Temporary Camp - Temporary camps are sites that were occupied for a short length of time (e.g., one day to one month) by a few people (from an individual to several families). These sites can be identified archaeologically by scattered artifacts, tool manufacturing debris, fire-affected rocks and possibly features. They differ from the first site type by size and frequency of cultural remnants. This type is somewhat a catch-all category. It includes sites that reflect a range of artifacts and/or cultural features that in combination do not allow the site to be typed in another category (e.g., pottery with flakes). The inferred function of the site is limited camping (i.e., limited subsistence and maintenance activities). However, an open site with any combination of flaked stone artifacts, ground stone, fire-affected rocks, and/or ceramics could fit in this site type.

03 Utilized Shelter or Cave - This site type represents archaeological sites found exclusively in rockshelters caves or under rock overhangs. If only rock art is present then the site is typed as 12 or 13. Three sub-types have been identified. These are as follows:

03a Occupation Rockshelter - This sub-type represents temporary or seasonal occupation locations containing cultural debris similar to that described for village locations (01) or temporary camps (02).

03b Transient Rockshelter - Rockshelter or overhang indicative of extremely limited use. The inferred use is that of overnight camping enroute to other locations. These sites are usually along an aboriginal trail or route of travel. Cultural remains may consist only of an isolated tool or a few flakes and possibly some fire-affected rocks. Absent from this type is a developed midden.

03c Storage Rock Shelter - Rockshelter or overhang, usually small in size, containing only basketry, pottery, or other cultural remains indicative of storage activities. This would include tool or food caches.

04 Milling Station - This site type is a manifestation of procurement and/or processing of hard (e.g., chia) and/or soft (e.g., acorn) seeds and other food items. Associated artifacts may include manos, metates, mortars or pestles. Bedrock mortars or bedrock metates (e.g., grinding slicks or rubs) may be present. This site type may consist of an isolated metate or a single bedrock metate or any combination of

artifacts or features indicative of milling activities. Associated with this site type may be an occasional flake or flaked stone tool.

05 Lithic Scatter - These sites are characterized exclusively by the presence of flaked stone tools, chipping waste, cores, retouched and utilized flakes, and/or flake material such as chalcedony, chert, jasper, opal, rhyolite, or obsidian. Other cultural material is absent. Since this general site type often constitutes a major percentage of the archaeological site inventory, five sub-types are used here to allow a closer assessment of this type's variability.

From the existing site record sheets, only the variables of 1) area and 2) density or quantity of flaked stone material present can be determined with any regularity. Giving two characteristics to each of the major variables, four combinations are possible.

The characteristics for area are simply 1) large, and 2) small. Large is considered to be greater than 50 square meters. Small is considered to be less than 50 square meters.

For density of quantity, the characteristics are 1) high, and 2) low. The determination of the characteristics is dependent on key terms used on the site record sheet or on the number of artifacts observed.

A high density is determined if terms such as "dense," "heavy," "thick," "numerous," "a wide variety," etc., are used in reference to quantity of flakes and/or flaked stone tools present. If only the number or a listing of flakes and/or flaked stone tools observed is given then a rough assessment of artifacts per ten square meters is made. Generally, an estimate of an average of more than 30 flakes and/or flaked stone tools per ten square meters is considered high.

A low density is determined if terms such as "thin," "few," "light," "small number," etc., are used in reference to quantity of flakes and/or flaked stone tools present. If only the number or a listing of flakes and/or flaked stone tools observed is given then a rough assessment of artifacts per ten square meters is made. Generally, an estimate of an average of less than 30 flakes and/or flaked stone tools per ten squre meters is considered low.

The four combinations of area and density are shown as follows:

DENSITY

		(+) High	(-) Low
Area	Large (+)	A + +	B + -
	Small (-)	C - +	D - -

-143-

The fifth sub-type, Chipping Circle, is a distinct archaeological feature which when occurring without other flaked stone material or flaked stone tools is recorded as an archaeological site.

The five sub-types of Lithic Scatters are briefly described as follows:

05a Large, Dense Lithic Scatter - A locus consisting of a high density of flakes and/or flaked stone tools over a large area (i.e., high density and large area).

05b Large, Light Lithic Scatter - A locus consisting of a low density of flakes and/or flaked stone tools over a large area (i.e., low density and large area).

05c Small, Dense Lithic Scatter A locus consisting of a high density of flakes and/or flaked stone tools over a small area (i.e., high density and small area).

05d Small, Light Lithic Scatter - A locus consisting of a low density of flakes and/or flaked stone tools over a small area (i.e., low density and small area).

05e Chipping Circle A loci consisting simply of a core with related flakes immediately around it. Occasionally, flakes from the core evidence possible utilization. Hammerstone(s) may on occasion be found in association. A "chipping circle" is usually only one or two meters in diameter. A cluster of chipping circles (i.e., two or more) may be considered a single site if they are less than 20 meters apart and more than 100 meters from another site. Occasionally, an isolated flake or flakedstone tool may be found in the vicinity of a chipping circle. If a chipping circle is associated with other flakes and/or flaked stone tools, or if it is part of a larger site, then another site type or sub-type is utilized.

06 Quarry - A quarry site is a location where lithic material has been extracted from a larger mass (usually crypto-crystalline), such as a seam, vein or outcrop, for the purpose of tool manufacture. Such sites are characterized by an abundance of flakes, cores, occasional hammerstones, preforms, blanks or rejects.

07 Pottery Scatter - This type of site is represented by surface scatters of pottery (ceramic) sherds or broken vessels. No other artifacts or features are present.

08 Cemetery - Prehistoric locations for human internment comprise this site type. Surface indications may include cairns, exposed bone, mounding or markers. This site type ranges from isolated burials in shallow holes to extensive cemeteries.

09 Cremation Locus - A special type of internment is the cremation. Charred human bone fragments may occasionally be found in small cavities in the rock, in dune areas, in utilized shelters or caves, or as part of camps or villages.

10 Intaglio - These are large figures produced on desert pavement surfaces in the form of animal, human, and geometric designs. Their distribution is usually limited to areas along the lower Colorado River or Yuha Desert but isolated occurrences in other areas have been noted.

11 Rock Alignment - Prehistoric alignments of cobbles and boulders occur in the California Desert. Such alignments vary in size and complexity ranging from simple lines to complex abstract or geometric designs.

12 Petroglyph Site - Petroglyphs represent pecked or incised figures or designs on boulders, rock outcrops or shelter walls.

13 Pictograph Site - Pictographs are painted figures or designs which occur most frequently on the walls of sheltered caves, boulders or outcrops. The most frequent colors are red, black and white although other colors such as orange, brown, yellow and green can occur.

>   Note: If both petroglyphs and pictographs are present then
>   the dominate rock art form (i.e., greatest number of
>   elements) dictates the site type to be given (e.g.,
>   petroglyph site with pictographs or pictograph site
>   with petroglyphs.) The lesser rock art form (i.e.,
>   smallest number of elements) is recorded as a cultural
>   feature.

14 Trail - Trails are marked routes of travel between permanent villages, temporary camps, and resource procurement areas. Where they survive, trails usually are faint linear impressions or clearings in the desert pavement or slight "shelves" along hillsides and canyon slopes. Potsherds and other artifacts may occur along trails, as might rock cairns or trail shrines. However, the trail is an entity in itself--a route of travel interlinking the various activity areas and sites of the aboriginal populations.

15 Roasting Pit - This site type encompasses the range of rock features which includes earth ovens, roasting pits and clusters of fire affected rock. This category is used when there is an absence of other cultural remains.

16 Isolated Find - An occurence of a single artifact or cultural features that does not conform to other site types are documented with this category. This includes isolated flaked stone tools, cores, manos, and other artifacts not covered by other site types (e.g., an isolated metate is included in 04). Cultural features included in this site type are single rock rings or single sleeping circles with no associated artifacts or other cultural features.

17 Cairn - Mounding of cobbles and/or boulders are found in the California Desert. These are referred to as rock cairns. Sometimes cairns mark trails, shrines, or burials. Cairns can appear singularly or in clusters.

B. HISTORICAL SITE TYPES. For purposes of this section, historic sites are defined as loci of past activity or activities of Hispanic and Euro-American populations. It includes sites documented in the historic record (i.e., diaries, historic accounts, andother historic documents) and sites for which no written record or reference can be found. The historic period in the study area dates back to 1776. At the other end, a site is normally considered "historic" if it is 40 years or older. However, more recent sites that have maintained historical integrity (e.g., homesteads) or are associated with a significant event or activity (e.g., WW II training camps) may also be included.

More than two dozen historical site types have been identified in localized areas within the California desert. These site types can be placed into five cultural categories which are indicative of general activities. These cultural categories or general activities are 1) Exploration, 2) Settlement 3) Military, 4) Mining, and 5) Transportation.

1. Exploration involves historical sites associated with early expeditions, explorations, immigrations, and government surveys. Sites associated with this category are simply campsites and routes of travel.

2. Settlement includes those sites indicative of living activities and maintenance activities associated with settlement. Sites within this category include town, hamlet, mining camp, dug out, homestead, farm, ranch, school, cemetery, well, trash dump, and other structures associated with settlement.

3. Military encompasses remnants of past military activities. Sites of this category are fort, camp, outpost, redoubt, and World War II training camp.

4. Mining is a category to cover activities specifically related to the extraction and processing of locatable, salable and/or hardrock minerals. Sites included in this category are mine, shaft, addit, tunnel, mill, arrastre, and mining works.

5. Transportation deals with historical sites that were involved with public conveyance of passengers and/or goods, especially for a commercial enterprise, and sites directly related to this activity. Sites within this category are pack trail, wagon road, stage route, early automobile road, railroad, railroad station and water stopovers.

The various site types are briefly described as follows:

01 Town - A compactly settled area usually larger than a hamlet.

02 Hamlet - A small settlement.

03 Mining Camp - A settlement associated specifically with mining activities. This is also indicative of much more transient use than either 01 or 02.

04 Homestead - A tract of land acquired from U.S. public lands by filing a record and living on and cultivating the tract.

05 Farm - A plot of land devoted to the raising of crops.

06 Ranch - A plot of land devoted to the raising of beef cattle and/or other livestock.

07 Railroad Station - The building, remains, and/or regularly scheduled stopping place of the train for the purpose of loading and unloading passengers and freight.

08 Post Office - A building and/or site once officially designated as a local branch of the U.S. Post Office.

09 School - A building used for educational instruction.

10 Structure - Something that is constructed (e.g., building) of rock, adobe, wood, or a combination of these materials or other material.

11 Fort - An official U.S. military designation for a permanent army post that is occupied continuously by troops.

12 Camp (1800's) - The lowest official U.S. military designation for an army post that is usually small but has a permanent detachment of men assigned to it.

13 Camp (WW II) - An official military post consisting mostly of tent structures and established as a base of operation for World War II training manuevers.

14 Outpost - An unofficial military designation used in the 1860's to identify a temporary post to which a small detachment of men (usually a non-commissioned officer and 3-10 enlisted men) from a regional camp were temporarily assigned.

15 Redoubt - A small, usually temporary, enclosed defensive work.

16 Mine - A pit or excavation in the earth from which mineral substances are taken.

17 Shaft - A vertical or inclined opening of uniform and limited cross section made for finding or mining ore.

18 Addit - A horizontal opening of uniform and limited cross section made for finding or mining ore.

19 Tunnel - A horizontal passageway through a ridge, hill or mountain and associated with mining activities.

20 Arrastre - A devise built to grind gold-bearing quartz. The early types consisted of a low stone and dirt wall built around a large and fairly level stone, hard pan or flat rock-lined floor.

A long horizontal beam was pivoted on a vertical post in the arrastre's center. One end of the beam was harnessed to a burro or mule to provide necessary power by walking in a circle outside the low arrastre wall. A heavy chain was fastened to the beam about midway, and the free end of the chain linked to a ring bolt wedged in a heavy drag stone(s).

21 Ore Mill - A site where crushing machinery, usually steam engine powered, was used to pulverize ore-bearing rock to facilitate the extraction of gold and/or other metals. Five- and ten-stamp mills were most common.

22 Mining Works An area where mining and/or processing works (e.g.; flumes, chutes, sorters, etc.) are present.

23 Dug Out - A shelter dug in a hillside or dug in the ground and roofed with sod or earth.

24 Railroad - The remains of a permanent road having a line of rails fixed to ties and laid on a roadbed or berm and providing tracks for railroad cars.

25 Automobile Road (Early) - Road used for early automobile travel (e.g., Model-T, etc.).

26 Wagon Road - Route habitually used by wagons pulled by draft animals.

27 Stage Route - Trail utilized regularly by the stagecoach companies for handling passengers and mail.

28 Pack Trail - Historic foot and pack animal (horse and mule) route of travel that was not used by wagons.

29 Exploration Route - Routes taken by early expeditions, explorers, travelers, and survey parties. Also included are routes used for domestic livestock drives.

30 Cemetery - A place with historic human internments associated with Euro-American activities (i.e., a historic burial ground).

31 Trash Dump - A place where refuse or other discarded materials are accumulated or dumped.

32 Well - A deep hole or shaft sunk into the earth to tap an underground supply of water.

33 Railroad Water Stop - A place along a railroad right-of-way where trains periodically stopped to take on water.

34 Isolated Find Singular occurance of a historic artifact such as the following:

Bottle
Stirrup
Horseshoe

Road grader